T H E

E S S E N T I A L

Freshwater Aquarium

Consulting Editor
BETSY SIKORA SIINO

Featuring Photographs by
AARON NORMAN

HOWELL
BOOK
HOUSE

Howell Book House
A Simon & Schuster Macmillan Company
1633 Broadway
New York, NY 10019

Macmillan Publishing books may be purchased for business or sales promotional use. For information please write: Special Markets Department, Macmillan Publishing USA, 1633 Broadway, New York, NY 10019.

Library of Congress Cataloging-in-Publication Data
The essential freshwater aquarium/featuring photographs by Aaron Norman
    p. cm.
  Includes bibliographical references and index
    ISBN 0-87605-331-2
    1. Aquariums   I. Norman, Aaron, 1929–   II. Howell Book House
SF457.E84   1998   98-3043
639.34—dc21   CIP

Manufactured in the United States of America
10 9 8 7 6 5 4 3 2

Series Directors: Dominique DeVito, Don Stevens
Series Editors: Jennifer Liberts, Amanda Pisani
Editorial Assistant: Michele Matrisciani
Photography Editor: Sarah Storey
Book Design: Paul Costello
Photography: All photography by Aaron Norman
Production Team: Heather Pope, Karen Teo, Chris Van Camp

CONTENTS

CHAPTER ONE: Fish Fundamentals 1

CHAPTER TWO: All About Aquariums 11

CHAPTER THREE: A Quality Home .38

CHAPTER FOUR: Freshwater Fish Families 47

CHAPTER FIVE: Choosing the Right Fish 53

CHAPTER SIX: Fish Nutrition 72

CHAPTER SEVEN: To Good Health .80

CHAPTER EIGHT: Resources 86

CHAPTER NINE: Recommended Reading 88

Index 90

Fish Fundamentals

The world of fish is both fascinating and complex. This book will help you understand this world and teach you what you need to know to successfully set up and maintain a freshwater aquarium. To do so, you will need a general knowledge of fish, their anatomy and biology, as well as a thorough understanding of their proper care. After taking a look at fish anatomy and what makes these animals so unique, this text will examine the aquarium and the importance of meeting the biological needs of fish.

FISH EVOLUTION

The group of aquatic animals that are known as fish has evolved for over 400 million years into the most numerous and diverse of the major vertebrate groups. Fish have permeated all the waters of the world,

Cherry Barb

adapting to an incredible variety of forms, lifestyles and behaviors in an equally diverse array of aquatic environments. From the seasonal freshwater streams, desert springs and salty bays to the coral reefs and deep open oceans, different species of fish have found and created suitable niches. There are well over 20,000 known species of fish that currently inhabit the earth and many more are being discovered every year.

Because salt water covers more than 70 percent of the earth's surface and fresh water only 1 percent, one would expect that there would be many more marine (saltwater) species than freshwater species of fish. Actually, 41 percent of the world's fish species inhabit strictly fresh water. Although quite similar in many ways to their marine counterparts, freshwater fish have adapted to a much wider range of habitats and to a greater variety of water conditions.

FISH BIOLOGY

Because there are no less than 8,000 kinds of freshwater fish, it is difficult to describe the "typical" fish. However, all fish have some common attributes. Water is 800 times denser than air, and fish have developed a variety of ways to move easily, breathe and feed in this dense medium. The biological adaptations that have developed for life under water include the body shape, fins, scales and swim bladder.

Body Shape

A great deal can be learned about a species of fish by looking at its body form or shape. Fish that are streamlined or bullet shaped are specially adapted to open waters, while flat or stocky fish are well adapted for living on or close to the bottom.

Fins

Almost all species of fish have fins in one form or another. The fins are critically important appendages that allow the fish to propel, stabilize, maneuver and stop. In some cases, fins have developed to protect the fish as well. Again, depending on the type of fish and the habitat in which it lives, the fins can take on many shapes and functions. Bottom, sedentary or slower moving fish possess rounded fins, while faster, open water fish generally have longer, pointed fins.

Fish scales are covered with a thin coating of mucus, which helps protect the fish from injury and infection. (Blue Rainbowfish)

3

Fins can be either paired or unpaired, depending on species and function. The pectoral fins are the paired fins closest to the head. These fins help the fish stabilize, turn, maneuver, hover and swim backwards. The pectoral fins are generally found just behind or below the gills on each side of the fish, under the midline of the body. The pelvic fins are also paired and are the most variable in position. In some fish, the pelvic fins lie under the fish toward the rear. In others, such as many tropical species, the pelvic fins are closer to the head under the pectorals. In general, the pelvic fins act as brakes while aiding in stabilizing and turning the fish.

The dorsal and anal fins are unpaired fins that are found protruding from the top and bottom of the fish behind the genital and anal openings, respectively. Dorsal fins may be elongated or short, elaborate or simple, singular or multiple. In some species of fish, the dorsal or anal fin may be completely lacking. Both fins help stabilize the fish and keep it moving straight. The caudal or tail fin is a single fin largely responsible for propelling the fish forward. This fin can also assist in turning and braking. Faster fish have deeply forked caudal fins while many deep-bodied and bottom fish have square or rounded tails.

In general, the main supporting structures of fish fins are soft rays. However, anyone who has handled a fish knows that the dorsal, anal or pectoral fins of many species also have spines. These sharp bony structures provide protection against predators.

Scales

The bodies of most tropical fish are covered with scales. The scales are composed of a hard bony substance and serve to protect the fish, reducing the chance of injury and infection. Covering the scales is a very thin layer of epidermal tissue that contains mucous cells. These cells produce the slimy texture that people normally attribute to fish. The mucous coating not only protects the fish from injury and infection but helps the fish swim more easily in the water, reducing friction between the body and water.

The scales of a fish are actually translucent and lack color. The vibrant colors of tropical fish are due to specialized pigment cells called chromatophores in the dermal layer of the skin. (Fish that are clear, like the Glassfish, lack these pigments.) The color of the fish depends on the types of chromatophores present. There are generally three types of chromatophores in fish: melanophores, xanthophores and iridophores. Melanophores give fish the darker colors of black, brown and blue; xanthophores produce the colors of red, yellow and orange; and iridophores reflect light, producing a silvery shine common to many fish.

Swim Bladder

As mentioned earlier, living in the dense medium of water presents a few problems for fish; one of these is buoyancy. Maintaining a certain level in the water column without having to expend a lot of energy is very important to fish. Therefore, most species have a special organ called the swim bladder. This gas-filled sac located in the abdominal cavity of the fish acts as a life vest, keeping the fish at the correct level in the water column. There are many types of swim bladders: The trout has a simple single-chambered sac, the goldfish a two-chambered type and the angelfish a three-chambered bladder. Different species also use different methods to fill the swim bladder with air.

Some have a direct connection between the esophagus and the bladder and simply swallow air to fill it. Others must rely on gas exchange from specialized blood vessels in the circulatory system to fill the bladder.

In addition to its role in buoyancy control, the swim bladder also helps to mechanically amplify sound for better hearing in certain species of fish.

Feeding

Just as a fish's body shape can tell you a lot about its swimming habits, its mouth can tell you something about its feeding habits. Bottom feeders have downward pointing mouths, while surface feeders have mouths that point upward. For most fish, the mouth is at the end of the snout. The size of the mouth is usually directly related to the size of the fish's preferred food. For example, large predatory fish like Oscars have larger oval mouths for consuming smaller fish. On the other hand, fish that normally feed on small aquatic invertebrates, like Neon Tetras, have smaller mouths. Some tropical freshwater fish have specialized mouths for specialized feeding

The angelfish's three-chambered swim bladder helps the fish maintain its position in the water column.

strategies. Plecostomus fish, for example, have special sucking-type mouths for bottom feeding.

Freshwater tropical fish have a relatively straightforward digestive system that varies from species to species. In general, food passes from the mouth, down the esophagus, to the stomach, through small and large intestines and the waste products are expelled through the anus. However, several species lack true

FISH ANATOMY

There are thousands of different species of fish, all uniquely adapted to their particular environments. However, most share fundamental characteristics that allow them to be classified together as fish.

Fins: Fins move the fish through the water, providing propulsion and steering.

Gills: Gills enable the fish to take in oxygen from the water.

Lateral Line: The lateral line is a sensory organ that alerts the fish to movement close by. It helps fish in schools to move in synchronization.

Scales: Scales streamline and protect the body of the fish as it moves through the water.

Swim Bladder: The swim bladder fills up with air, thereby controlling the fish's level in the water column.

stomachs and instead have elongated, supercoiled intestines.

Breathing

Among the most primary of the basic needs of fish is oxygen. Like land animals, fish require oxygen to live. However, fish must derive oxygen from water and have specialized organs, called gills, that allow them to do so. The gills of a fish are analogous to our lungs: They supply oxygen and remove carbon dioxide from the blood of the fish. Oxygen is then transported by the blood to the tissues where it is used in the body's energy-making process.

Most fish have four gills on each side of the head protected by a single gill flap, or operculum. When a fish breathes, water is taken into the mouth and passed over the gills and out the operculum. As water passes over the membranes and filaments of the gills, oxygen is removed and carbon dioxide is excreted. The gills have a very high number of blood vessels that deliver the oxygen to the rest of the fish's body.

Aside from the notable exceptions outlined above, fish typically possess the general circulatory, digestive, respiratory and nervous system features common to most vertebrates. Curious fish keepers should examine the books listed in chapter 9 for more detailed descriptions of the unique anatomy of fish.

Senses

With few exceptions, fish have no less than five senses that they use to

feed, avoid predators, communicate
and reproduce.

SIGHT

The eyes of most fish are similar to
our own, except that they lack eyelids and their irises work much more
slowly. Rapid changes in light inten-
sity tend to shock a fish, a fact that
should be taken into account by the
aquarist. Gradual changes in light
allow the fish to accommodate and
avoid temporary blindness. The
location of the spherical lenses of
fish eyes renders most fish near-
sighted. Fish can detect color,
although the ability to do so varies
from species to species.

SOUND

Water is a much more efficient con-
ductor of sound than air is.
Therefore, sound carries much far-
ther and faster in water than in air.
Most fish do not possess external
ears, but rather an inner ear structure not noticeable on the outside of
the fish. The auditory component of
the inner ear consists of the sacculus
and the lagena, which house the
sensory components of hearing, the
otoliths. Sound vibrations pass
through the water, through the fish
and reverberate the otoliths in the

inner ear. As mentioned previously,
in some cases, the swim bladder
articulates with the ear to amplify
sound. Hearing is an integral component in the life of a fish.

SMELL

A fish has external nasal passages
called nares that allow water to pass
into and out of the olfactory organ
located above its mouth and below
its eyes. Water flows through the
nares and into the olfactory pits
where odors are perceived and com-
municated to the brain via a large
nerve. The olfactory system of the
fish is not attached to the respiratory system like it is in humans, but
remains isolated from the mouth

*Except for their
lack of eyelids, a
fish's eyes have
much in com-
mon with those
of a human.
(Tinfoil Barb)*

and gills. For fish, smell is particularly important for use in prey and mate detection.

TASTE

The sense of taste is generally a close range sense in fish and is especially helpful in the identification of both food and noxious substances. In addition to being located in the mouth, the taste buds are located on several external surfaces such as the fish's skin, lips and fins. Catfish have specialized barbels with taste buds that help them detect food items in murky waters.

TOUCH

Fish have very specialized organs comprising the lateral line system that allow them to detect water movements. Sensory receptors lying along the surface of the fish's body in low pits or grooves detect water displacement. The lateral line is easily visible along the sides of most fish. This unique system helps the fish detect other fish and avoid obstacles.

FISH IN CAPTIVITY

It is no surprise that man has favored keeping fish in captivity for

This Barred Shovelnose Catfish has a mouth specifically adapted for life as a bottom-feeder.

centuries. The Chinese kept the common goldfish as far back as A.D. 265. Care and husbandry of fish have come a long way over the centuries, and in recent years there has been an incredible explosion in fish culture.

There was a time when most tropical freshwater fish kept in captivity were taken from their native habitats. This practice contributed to the degradation of tropical habitats and the local depletion of many species. Fortunately, modern husbandry techniques have taken the tremendous pressure off natural stocks; now, many of the common aquarium species are bred in captivity. Selective breeding has also allowed for the rearing of hardier fish that are more adaptable to the varying water conditions of the aquarium.

The Fish Keeper's Responsibilities

Fish in their natural environment are subjected to many challenges. Most of these involve natural processes of predation, feeding, reproduction and disease. Natural catastrophic events that alter water quality are rare, and fish can generally avoid them by moving to other areas. Fish in their natural habitats are usually very much responsible for their own well-being—when they are hungry, they seek out food; when the environment becomes hostile, they move to an area that is more hospitable. (A possible exception to this would be fish living in areas assaulted by man-made pollution.)

Fish maintained in an artificial environment are also faced with

THE FISH KEEPER'S RESPONSIBILITIES

The fish keeper (that's you) has an obligation to care for the fish he or she has brought home. Because the fish are contained in an artificial environment, it is up to you to establish and maintain their living space in an appropriate manner. The fish keeper is responsible for providing:

- high water quality
- proper feeding
- correct water temperature
- a balanced fish community of the proper density
- appropriate habitat and shelter
- sufficient lighting

Make sure you are ready to accept these responsibilities and the daily chores that go with them before you start setting up your aquarium.

survival challenges. However, in the confines of the aquarium, most of these challenges cannot be met by the fish and must instead be met by the fish keeper. When you take it upon yourself to set up an aquarium, you are accepting the responsibility of meeting all of the needs of its inhabitants. The aquarist is responsible for maintaining good water quality and correct water temperature and for providing proper nutrition and a balanced fish community of the proper density. He must also provide an appropriate habitat, shelter and sufficient lighting. The fish are totally dependent upon the keeper to meet their everyday and emergency needs. As you gain experience as a fish keeper, you may go beyond the basic needs and try to breed your fish or establish specialty tanks. But first, it's important to start slowly with your aquarium and develop your talents as an aquarist; you will learn a tremendous amount through your own experiences.

Find a Good Dealer

Before you purchase your aquarium supplies and fish, try to visit all the local aquarium stores and choose one or two to work with. It is very important to establish a good working relationship with your aquatic dealer because you will need someone to advise you during the setup and maintenance of your system. You want somebody who maintains a good clean business, has healthy fish and is always willing to take time to answer your questions. A good dealer will give you invaluable information on new and reliable products. Choose someone with the right attitude, who will be consistently available to help. Try to avoid dealers who will not take the time to explain things to you or to net the specific fish you desire. Larger dealers with many employees may not meet your needs as a beginner. I've always preferred the smaller pet shops with knowledgeable staff members who cater to the needs of all levels of experience, are willing to special order supplies and would rather send you elsewhere than sell you an improper choice. When you settle on one or two dealers, you are ready to begin planning your aquarium.

CHAPTER TWO

All About Aquariums

THE RIGHT TANK

Before you bring your aquarium home, determine where you are going to put it. To avoid excess heat and algal growth, do not place the aquarium in direct sunlight. Make sure that the structure that the aquarium will rest on will hold the weight of the full aquarium. Water weighs about 8.4 pounds per gallon, so a 30-gallon tank will weigh at least 250 pounds when full. Choose a location that has an adequate electrical supply and is not too far from a source of water. Well-used living areas provide excellent settings for aquariums because the fish acclimate to people entering and leaving the room. Placing the aquarium in a rarely used area will render the fish skittish and timid when people approach. Lastly, choose a location that can tolerate a water spill. Even the most meticulous of aquarists may spill water around an aquarium, and in many cases water will be splashed from a tank. Be thoughtful in your decision as to where the tank will be because once the aquarium is set up, it cannot be easily moved.

Agassiz' Dwarf Cichlid

What Size Tank?

The general rule of thumb is to buy the largest aquarium that you can afford and accommodate in your home. The reason for this is fairly straightforward. Fish require adequate space to swim and sufficient oxygen to live; both are dictated by the size of the tank. The oxygen content of water is related to the surface area of the tank and the temperature of the water. Warmer water has less oxygen than colder water. Because most freshwater tropical fish prefer water warmer than 75°F, the amount of oxygen may be limited in the tank. The more surface area a tank has, the more room for gas exchange at the surface—more opportunity for oxygen to enter the water and toxic gases to leave. Therefore, the larger the surface area of the tank, the more fish the tank can hold.

The number of fish you can keep in your aquarium is also determined by the surface area of your tank. Calculate the surface area of the tank by multiplying the length times the width. This number will tell you the maximum inches of fish that your aquarium can accommodate. Most fish keepers generally contend that 1 inch of coldwater fish requires 30 square inches of surface area and 1 inch of tropical water fish requires 12 square inches of surface area. (Coldwater fish generally have higher oxygen requirements than tropical fish, thus the difference in space requirements.) For example, if you have space in your living room for a 30-gallon aquarium with a length of 32 inches and a width of 14 inches, then you will have a surface area of 448 square inches (32 × 14). This tank has the capacity for 15 ($^{448}/_{30}$) inches of coldwater fish or 37 ($^{448}/_{12}$) inches of warmwater fish. In real terms, you could put seven 2-inch goldfish, which are considered coldwater fish, or 37 1-inch Neon Tetras, which are warmwater fish, in this tank. Of course, you will probably want to mix several species of fish of varying lengths in the tank. The minimal starter tank should be a 20-gallon aquarium.

Because surface area is so important to the capacity and health of your aquarium, long tanks are much better than tall tanks. Even though both tanks may hold the same volume of water, the upright (tall) tank will have a much lower carrying capacity of fish because of its smaller surface area.

Once you have decided on the appropriate size of your aquarium, choosing the tank itself is very straightforward.

Most home aquariums are constructed of rectangular glass plates sealed with a silicone rubber cement. These are by far the most common and practical aquariums to buy and are recommended for the beginner. They are built for the sole purpose of housing living animals and are, therefore, nontoxic. Glass does not scratch as easily as acrylic nor does it yellow as acrylic does. Aquariums with plastic or metal frames are sometimes available, but these designs are not typically as aesthetically pleasing and the frames are usually unnecessary. When choosing your tank, be sure that there are no scratches on the glass and that there are no gaps in the silicone that may cause leakage.

A brief mention of the fish bowl will hopefully prevent the beginner from buying one. The confined, inhumane fish bowl is not a proper environment for a fish, whether it's a goldfish or any other freshwater fish. Water in a fish bowl is unfiltered, not properly aerated and very poorly maintained. A fish bowl is no more an aquarium than a closet is a house.

Surface area is an extremely important consideration when purchasing a tank. The surface-to-air ratio of the tank is much larger than that of a bowl.

The Aquarium Stand

The best support for the heavy weight of the aquarium and all its components is a commercially manufactured aquarium stand. This type of support is built to hold a full aquarium. Homemade stands and other furniture may look sturdy, but can fail under the heavy load. Stand failure can be costly to both the aquarist and the homeowner, not to mention the fish, so don't try to save money on your support for the aquarium.

If you don't buy a commercially built stand, it is recommended that you place a $5/8$-inch sheet of plywood and a $1/2$-inch sheet of polystyrene (cut to the dimensions of the tank) under the tank. These layers will even out any imperfections in the

13

supporting surface and distribute the load of the tank.

The Hood

An essential item for any aquarium is a hood or cover. This important piece of equipment performs a variety of functions. It prevents unwanted items from entering the tank and injuring the fish. It also prevents overzealous fish from jumping out of the tank. Remember, fish cannot breathe air, and nothing is worse than finding your pet on the floor next to the aquarium in the morning. The cover prevents water from splashing onto the walls and floor, causing damage, and it slows the rate of water evaporation from the tank. Water will condense on the cover and reenter the tank instead of evaporating, which reduces the necessity of adding more water. In addition, the hood helps the aquarium retain heat, thereby reducing the use of the heating unit. Lastly, the hood keeps water from damaging the aquarium light and prevents a potentially dangerous electrical problem.

The hood is generally fitted to the dimensions of the tank and is adjustable to allow for aquarium

accessories. It should be composed of thick ($\frac{1}{8}$-inch) glass or plastic so it can support the weight of other aquarium components if needed. It should be segmented so the entire assembly need not be removed to feed the fish or work in the tank. For the beginner, the type of hood that also contains the aquarium light is strongly recommended. These units are self-contained and designed to keep water from the lighting unit, minimize danger and cover the entire tank. If possible, the tank, stand and hood should be purchased as a package from a single manufacturer. This prevents the problem of mismatching aquarium components and may also be less expensive than purchasing components separately.

CREATING PROPER WATER CONDITIONS

The most important requirement for maintaining healthy fish is clean water. Fish in a natural environment are generally exposed to an open system of freshwater continuously; products of respiration and digestion are swept away and naturally filtered. In contrast, fish housed in the aquarium live in a closed system where products of respiration and digestion remain until they are removed. The fish keeper must take responsibility for removal of these wastes and maintaining clean water. The all-important piece of equipment that removes toxic substances from the aquarium is the filter.

Freshwater fish have adapted to a wide variety of habitats around the world. The water in each of these places has its own chemical characteristics to which the species of fish living there have adapted. These characteristics of water include pH (acidity level), hardness (mineral content), temperature and oxygen content. In many cases, fish that have adapted to a specific temperature or pH cannot readily live under different conditions.

The pH scale, which identifies the acidity of the water, ranges from 0 to 14. A pH of 7 is neutral, a pH of 1 is very acidic and a pH of 14 is very alkaline. This scale is logarithmic, meaning that each number is ten times stronger than the preceding number. For example, a pH of 2 is ten times more acidic than a pH of 3 and one hundred times more acidic than a pH of 4.

A variety of factors influence the pH of the water, including the

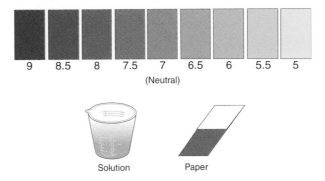

9   8.5   8   7.5   7   6.5   6   5.5   5
(Neutral)

Solution   Paper

amount of carbon dioxide and fish wastes present. In general, the beginner's aquarium pH should be between 6.5 and 7.5. Commercial test kits that are very simple to use are available at most pet stores. The pH level should be monitored every week or two to detect any changes. An abrupt drop in pH may be indicative of an increase in carbon dioxide or fish wastes. An increase in aeration or partial water change may alleviate the problem.

There are methods available to alter pH in the aquarium. However, unless you are attempting to attain specific pH levels as dictated by the special needs of certain species of fish, it is not typically recommended that you use them. Readers who are interested in these techniques should refer to Chapter 9, "Recommended Reading."

Determining the pH of the water in your aquarium can be done with simple testing kits available at pet stores. Results may look something like this.

15

Water Hardness

The amount of dissolved mineral salts in the water, namely calcium and magnesium, is referred to as its hardness. Water with high concentrations of salts is referred to as "hard," while low levels create "soft" water. The degree of hardness scale (dH) ranges from 0 to over 30 degrees with 4–8 degrees representing soft water and 18–30 degrees representing hard water. Most freshwater fish do best in water between 3 and 14 degrees of hardness. The beginner generally does not need to alter water hardness unless the local tap water is excessively hard or soft. Commercial kits are now available to test and alter the degree of water hardness. These too can be purchased at a pet store.

The Nitrogen Cycle

Fish are living creatures that obtain energy from food and burn that energy with the help of oxygen that they breathe from the water. These processes generate waste products that are returned to the environment via the gills and the anus. These wastes are primarily carbon dioxide and nitrogenous compounds like ammonia. In the aquarium, these

wastes must be removed. Carbon dioxide generally leaves the water through aeration at the surface or through photosynthesis by aquarium plants. Toxic nitrogenous compounds are converted to less toxic compounds via the nitrogen cycle.

In nature, the nitrogen cycle involves the conversion of toxic nitrogenous wastes and ammonia into harmless products by bacterial colonies. In short, species of bacteria convert solid wastes excreted by fish into ammonia, ammonia into nitrite and nitrite into nitrate. Nitrate is then utilized by plants as fertilizer and removed from the water. A healthy aquarium depends greatly on the nitrogen cycle to reduce toxic ammonia into less toxic nitrogen compounds.

Filter Systems

In natural systems, nitrogen compounds are readily removed from the fish's habitat. In the aquarium, this is accomplished by the filtration system. There are three basic types of filtration: mechanical, chemical and biological.

Mechanical filters physically remove suspended particles from the water by passing it through a fine filter medium that sifts out the particles. External power filters and canister filters provide rapid mechanical filtration. Chemical filtration involves the chemical treatment of water to remove toxic substances. When you add activated carbon to an external power filter, you are providing chemical filtration. Biological filtration utilizes the nitrogen cycle to remove toxic compounds from the water. An excellent example of a biological filter is the undergravel filter, which draws water through the aquarium substrate. This substrate contains the necessary bacteria to convert nitrogenous wastes to nitrate. Although this type of filtration requires a bit of time to establish a viable working bacteria colony, it provides the best kind of filtration.

Most commercially manufactured aquarium filters provide all three kinds of filtration. For example, the external power filter will mechanically remove particles, chemically remove toxins if it contains activated carbon and biologically convert nitrogenous wastes via the nitrogen cycle in its filter media.

Some types of filters available to the beginner include the internal box filter, the external power filter, the external canister filter and the undergravel filter. These are certainly not the only types of filters available, but they are the most common. Choosing the right one for your new aquarium can be a bit confusing, given all the different types and manufacturers. Here is a brief

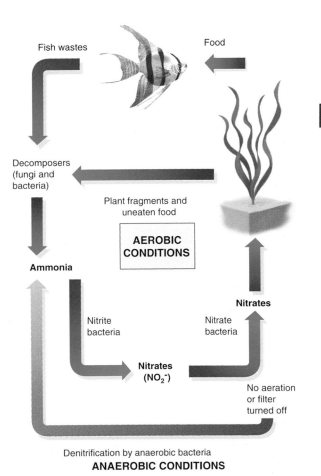

The nitrogen cycle.

Fish wastes

Food

Decomposers
(fungi and
bacteria)

Plant fragments and
uneaten food

AEROBIC
CONDITIONS

Ammonia

Nitrite
bacteria

Nitrate
bacteria

Nitrates

**Nitrates
(NO$_2^-$)**

No aeration
or filter
turned off

Denitrification by anaerobic bacteria
ANAEROBIC CONDITIONS

17

Maintaining a healthy aquarium requires investing in certain crucial pieces of equipment such as a good tank, filter and aeration systems, plants and decorations.

description of each type with the advantages and disadvantages.

INTERNAL BOX FILTER

As the name implies, the internal box filter sits inside the aquarium. An external air pump drives air through the box, drawing water from the aquarium through fibrous filter media and activated charcoal. Layers of filter media provide mechanical and chemical filtration as well as adequate substrate for biological filtration. Because it is driven by air, this filter circulates and aerates the water. Nonetheless, the box filter does not provide adequate levels of

filtration for the average aquarium. Aquarists who start with a tank of 20 gallons or more should not use this type of filter system to provide filtration. It is simply too small to handle the waste and debris that accumulate in the tank and would have to be changed frequently.

EXTERNAL POWER FILTERS

The external power filter is the easiest and least complicated filter system for the beginning aquarist to employ. These filters provide all three kinds of filtration and are specifically designed to turn over large amounts of water. The external power filter hangs on the side of the tank and is powered by its own motor. Water is drawn into the filter by a U-shaped siphon tube; it passes over layers of fibrous filter material and activated carbon. Water is returned to the tank via a gravity trickle system or a return pipe. While it works on the same premise as the box filter, the power filter is much more efficient at removing waste and debris from the tank. It does not need to be cleaned as frequently as the box filter. Newer models have specialized filter cartridges that make cleaning these filters extremely easy. In addition, various types of cartridges can be purchased to chemically alter water quality and correct water chemistry problems. Like the box filter, the power filter circulates the water, providing aeration.

The external canister filter is the next "step up" in power filters. This filter is much larger than the others and is designed to filter large tanks of 50 gallons or more. The canister filter is composed of a large jarlike canister that generally sits next to the tank. It contains filter media and activated carbon like the other filters but has a much more powerful

motor for filtering large amounts of water. Water is drawn by an intake suction line and sent back to the aquarium through a return line. Water circulation can be provided by these filters if the return line is properly positioned. However, this kind of filter is recommended for the aquarist with the larger tank.

UNDERGRAVEL FILTER

The undergravel filter is considered by many to be the most effective type of filter because it provides biological filtration. This filter consists of a plastic plate that sits under the gravel of the tank. Water is drawn through the gravel by pumping air to the bottom of the filter with an external air pump. Some undergravel filters are driven by powerheads mounted on the intake tubes. Both types provide excellent water circulation and aeration. In essence, this filter uses the aquarium gravel itself as the filter media. Thus, very little mechanical filtration is involved and chemical filtration is completely lacking. The undergravel filter relies chiefly on the establishment of a healthy bacterial colony in the gravel. For this reason, certain kinds of gravel are required for this filter and a longer setup time of many weeks is

It is important to learn about the water conditions fish require before you attempt to start an aquarium.

necessary to establish bacterial colonies. However, once a healthy filtration system is established, this filter can be used for months without intense maintenance and cleaning. Although this system provides the most valuable kind of filtration, it may be the most complicated for the beginner. Excessive debris in the aquarium can clog the filter bed and must be removed routinely. Aquarists who want to maintain live plants will find that this filter will destroy root systems. In addition, fish may disturb the substrate and upset the filtration bed as well. The novice is better off with an external power filter before tackling the complexities of the undergravel filter system.

Aeration

Although most filters provide water circulation and aeration to the aquarium, it is a very good idea to have an external air pump moving air through one or more airstones in the tank. Fish need to have a plentiful supply of oxygen available for respiration. This is especially true for tanks that are at their fullest carrying capacity of fish. The air pump will increase circulation in the tank, promote oxygen exchange at the surface, increase the escape of carbon dioxide and carbon monoxide and free ammonia from the tank. In addition, this increase in circulation will mix all the aquarium levels so that a uniform temperature is maintained throughout the tank.

AIR PUMPS

There are two general air pump designs: the diaphragm type and the piston type. The former is much more common and will generally provide enough maintenance-free usage for the beginner's aquarium. The piston pump, however, is more powerful and should be used in larger aquariums and if an undergravel filter and multiple airstones need to be powered. The size and power output of air pumps vary. Consult your local dealer to match your aquarium with the proper air pump.

AIRSTONES

The airstone is generally made of porous rock that allows air to pass through it, splitting the airstream into tiny bubbles. Too fine a mist will cause bubbles to adhere to various tank decorations and to fish. You want the bubbles to travel slowly to the surface and agitate the water. Commercially manufactured tank decorations that

act as airstones can be purchased at most pet stores.

AIR HOSE

Your air pump and airstones will require an air hose to form the link between the two. This is plastic tubing that will deliver air from your pump to the airstone. The hose should fit snugly at all joints so that air does not escape from the system. Air leaks will reduce the efficiency of the system (filter, airstone) and may ultimately burn out the pump. Make sure that the tubing is manufactured for use in the aquarium; other grades may be toxic to fish.

If you intend to run multiple airstones or additional devices like filters from a single pump, you will need one or more air valves. These will enable air flow to be directed to multiple devices from a single pump. The use of several air valves will allow you to turn devices on and off as you see fit.

The Heater

Based on their temperature preference, fish can be grouped in two general categories. Temperate fish include many species that inhabit cooler waters. However, the fish most commonly seen in the fresh-water aquarium belong to tropical species. The term tropical refers to natural habitats where the waters are warm throughout the year.

It should come as no surprise, therefore, that it is necessary to maintain your aquarium within a specific temperature range. This is the job of the aquarium heater. This essential piece of equipment will maintain your tank at a constant temperature regardless of the room temperature.

With the exception of a few fish like the common goldfish, the species you will be keeping as a beginner will require that the aquarium temperature be maintained at 75° to 79°F (24° to 26°C). However, the proper temperature is entirely species dependent, and you should consult your local pet dealer or one of the many fish encyclopedias (see the bibliography in chapter 9) for specific temperature requirements. Obviously, you should not mix species that have very different temperature preferences.

There are a few types of aquarium heaters available to the aquarist, but the most common is the submersible glass tubular heater with a built-in thermostat. This heater attaches to the side of the tank and has external controls. Once it is properly set, it will automatically respond to changes in water temperature and turn on and off. If one of these is to be used, it is recommended that the aquarist double-check the accuracy of the dial with a thermometer.

In general, you should place your heater close to an area of high circulation so heated water can be rapidly and evenly distributed throughout the tank. A good location is usually near the filter system or the airstones. The fully submersible heater can be placed at the bottom of the tank so heating convection can be optimized.

Heater size is largely dependent on the size of the aquarium. The general rule is 5 watts of power for every gallon of water. Thus, a 20-gallon tank would require a 100-watt heater. Many fish keepers recommend that two heaters be used in aquariums over 50 gallons; this allows for a more even distribution of heat in the aquarium and will also maintain correct temperatures if one heater fails. The calculated wattage should be divided between the heaters (50 gallons would require two 125-watt heaters).

As with all electrical components, please handle your heater with extreme care. Do not switch your submersible heater on until it is submersed in water. Keep all of your electrical components unplugged until the tank is completely set up and full.

Thermometer

In order to maintain your temperature at suitable levels, all aquarists need an accurate thermometer. There are basically two types of thermometers for the aquarium: the internal floating or fixed thermometer and the external stick-on thermometer. The former type tends to be more accurate—the latter has a tendency to read a few degrees too low. This piece of equipment is of the utmost importance to the aquarium, yet is not expensive. Having two thermometers is beneficial because it allows you to carefully monitor your aquarium temperature as well as to compare the accuracy of each unit. Don't cut corners when it comes to maintaining water quality and water temperature.

AQUARIUM LIGHTING

Proper lighting is a necessary component for every aquarium because it provides illumination and promotes plant growth. While lighting from the sun provides a natural setting, it will also promote excessive algal growth and alter temperature, so aquariums should be placed away from sunlit areas. Instead, beginning aquarists should purchase a commercially manufactured aquarium light to illuminate the tank. Like all aquarium components, these come in a variety of types and forms. By far the most common is the fluorescent light that fits snugly on top of the aquarium hood and evenly provides cool illumination.

There are several types of fluorescent bulbs that can be purchased to create special effects in your aquarium. If you intend to maintain plants, fluorescent tubes are available that cover the ideal spectral range of plants and promote plant growth. For example, red and blue colored light will enhance the colors of red and blue fish while promoting plant growth. Your pet shop dealer will carry a full variety of fluorescent

It's best to use artificial lighting rather than natural light to illuminate your aquarium; sunlight will promote the excessive growth of algae.

light bulbs. If you purchase your fish tank with a hood and light canopy, as is recommended for beginners, the latter will most often be a fluorescent light. If you do not purchase a tank, cover and light package, make sure that the light that you buy extends the entire length of the tank. This is by far the most efficient and economical form of lighting available for your tank and is the most highly recommended for the beginner.

When choosing your lighting, you must consider the depth of your aquarium and the number of live plants that you intend to grow.

These two aspects of your tank will dictate the power, number and type of bulbs that you will purchase. The general rule is 2–2.5 watts per gallon of water. However, if you intend to maintain large numbers of live plants, you should consult some of the sources listed in the bibliography before purchasing your lighting system.

An often overlooked component to the lighting system is an on/off time switch. Tropical freshwater fish come from regions where daylight lengths range from ten to fifteen hours. A time switch will automatically turn on and shut off your

lighting system so that a consistent day length can be maintained. A twelve-hour day is generally recommended for most community aquariums. With regard to lighting, efforts should be made to keep from startling fish; avoid suddenly switching the light on or off. To better simulate a normal sunset, you should switch off the aquarium light about an hour before other room lights are turned off. This little detail will help keep your fish happy and well adjusted.

INSIDE THE TANK

Your community aquarium will feature a variety of fish from multiple habitats, and it is best to create an aquascape that is pleasing to the fish as well as to the human eye. This will require a variety of components that meet the habitat needs of its inhabitants.

Gravel

The bottom substrate of your aquarium will consist of gravel. The gravel is a natural addition that provides anchorage to plants and other decorations and also provides a home for useful bacteria that power the

nitrogen cycle and rid the aquarium of toxic wastes. The beginner should be careful when choosing a substrate for the new aquarium. Certain kinds of materials can alter the chemistry of the aquarium, creating water hardness problems. For this reason, the beginner should not collect gravel or other aquarium fixtures from the wild, but rather purchase them from a pet dealer. As you develop a better understanding of the water hardness in your locality and its effects on your aquarium, you will be able to add more natural components.

All aquarium stores sell gravel for the freshwater aquarium. Be sure not to purchase coral sand, which is recommended for saltwater aquarium use only. Gravel comes in a variety of sizes ranging from coarse to very fine. If you intend to use an undergravel filter, very fine gravel will clog it and compromise its effectiveness. It will also harm the mouths and digestive systems of bottom feeding fish. On the other hand, if grains are too large, fish that tend to dig will not be able to move the substrate. This is particularly important for successfully breeding fish. A good medium pea-size gravel is well suited for the

Plants

The first decision you must make in regard to plants is whether to add artificial or live plants to your aquarium. Because the beginning aquarist is faced with a variety of problems in the first year of maintaining an aquarium, the maintenance and nurturing of live plants need not be added to the list of things that can go wrong. Although live plants are more visually appealing than artificial plants and provide an excellent service of reducing carbon dioxide and utilizing nitrates in the tank, they also have very specific needs that must be met. If proper care is not taken, they will die and contribute to water quality problems that you are desperately trying to avoid.

If you choose to install artificial plants, there are a great many varieties from which to select. The more expensive forms look like real plants and give the added effect of having plant life in your aquarium without the risk of degrading water quality.

If you want to graduate to live plants or pursue live plants from the onset, it is important to have an understanding of plants and the kinds available to the freshwater

A wide variety of colors will make choosing the right gravel an exciting part of decorating your aquarium.

beginner's aquarium. Gravel also comes in a variety of colors ranging from bright reds to natural tones of gray. Which color or colors to use is a matter of individual taste, but keep in mind the color of lighting that you will be using when choosing your gravel colors.

The gravel should be about $1^{1}/_{2}$–2 inches deep on the aquarium bottom. If you use an undergravel filter, $2^{1}/_{2}$–3 inches is recommended. It is always best to buy a bit extra so that when you aquascape your tank, you have sufficient amounts to sculpt the bottom.

aquarist. Plants remove carbon dioxide and add oxygen to the water during photosynthesis and utilize nitrates generated by the nitrogen cycle. However, to do so, plants require sufficient amounts of light. In low light or in darkness plants do not photosynthesize; instead they produce carbon dioxide like fish. This will influence the aquarium pH and overall water quality. That is why it is very important to provide adequate illumination and sufficient filtration if live plants are added to the tank.

Plants will add an additional source of food for fish that browse on vegetable matter or feed on algal colonies that develop on the plants' leaves. In addition, plants are a good indicator of the health of your aquarium, as they are the first to die if anything goes awry.

According to Barry James, author of *A Fishkeeper's Guide to Aquarium Plants,* aquatic plants can be divided into several types based on their form, size and growing characteristics.

Floating plants float on or just below the surface; their root system dangles in the water. These plants provide shade to other plants and fish in the aquarium. A common species of floating plant is *Riccia fluitans,* which is fast growing and provides an ideal spawning habitat.

Bunch plants reproduce off a single stem and quickly envelop a tank. The long stems and leaves arranged in pairs or whorls make these plants ideal for planting as a background in the aquarium. *Egeria densa* is a bunch plant that is great for beginners. It grows fast, cleans the water and produces a lot of oxygen. *Vallisneria spiralis,* another bunch type plant that is very hardy, grows to about 15 inches and spreads rapidly in dense clumps.

Specimen plants are larger plants that should be planted in the middleground to create a striking design. Popular species of specimen plants include the Amazon Sword Plant, *Echinodorus* species, extremely tolerant plants with leaves that are broad in the middle and tapered at each end.

Deep marginal plants grow from bulbs or tubers and produce long stems. They are ideal plants for the middleground, background or back corners of the tank. Species of *Nymphaea* and *Aponogeton* are ideal deep marginal plants that have modest care requirements. The former, however, are water lilies that

27

tend to block out light from the other plants if allowed to grow unchecked.

Middleground plants in the form of rosettes are similar to but smaller than specimen plants. These include *Cryptocoryne affinis,* which grows to only 12 inches and is very suitable for grouping. *Cryptocoryne* species are slow growers and take time to establish themselves. They are also easily affected by disease and sometimes require iron supplements.

Lastly, foreground plants are small plants ideally suited to the foreground of the tank. These include *Eleocharis* species with their bunched grasslike appearance.

Certainly, this is just a smattering of the species of plants that are available in most pet stores. If you are interested in maintaining live plants in a new aquarium, consult the references listed in the bibliography (chapter 9) before proceeding to select a plant species.

Just as different species of fish have specific temperature and water quality requirements, so do the various species of plants. The species outlined above are well suited to the aquarium of the novice aquarist. However, aquariums with live plants

generally require more light than those with artificial plants. This must be considered when setting up the aquarium. In addition, plants generally do better in finer substrate than that recommended for the average community tank. This too should be taken into account when selecting the types of fish that will inhabit your tank.

Just as you should spend time selecting your fish, select your plants carefully. Make sure that the root system looks healthy and that the leaves are free of brown decay before buying the plant. Get to know a little about each plant species, its maximum size and light and water type requirements. You don't want to add a plant that will outgrow or overly shade your aquarium.

Be sure to take proper care of your plants once they are added to your aquarium. Some species require routine fertilization. This can be accomplished by using commercially available liquid, tablet and substrate fertilizers. Be sure to read the instructions carefully, as the frequency and amount of fertilization depends on which product you purchase. In addition to fertilizer, routine cleaning of plants is essential.

Live plants add natural beauty and a beneficial source of nutrition to your aquarium, but you must be sure to keep them clean and healthy.

About once a week remove dead leaves from plants by hand. This will prevent debris from degrading water quality and inhibiting photosynthesis. Depending on how fast your plants grow, you will need to frequently trim and prune them to prevent them from overgrowing your aquarium. Remember, plants utilize oxygen at night and will, therefore, be competing with your fish for oxygen if the plants dominate the tank.

Decorations

Pet stores sell a variety of tank decorations that enhance the habitat you are providing for your fish. Some come in the forms of plastic or ceramic creations and others are simply attractive rocks and stones. By purchasing these tank decorations from your reputable dealer, you are avoiding contaminating your tank with toxic substances and water chemistry-modifying agents. Avoid

Your fish will appreciate the presence of a few decorative items that add shelter as well as visual variety.

the temptation to collect your own rocks until you know how to identify each kind and know the influence that they may have on your aquarium.

Before buying any decorations for your aquarium, take the time to design the kind of setting you want to build for your fish. In their natural habitats, fish have access to shelter as well as sufficient swimming space. Caves and rock ledges for the fish to hide in will mimic your fishes' natural habitat and increase their sense of security and well-being.

OTHER ACCESSORIES

As you develop your talents as an aquarist, you will begin to accumulate many accessories for your tank that make your job easier and help you maintain a happy, healthy aquarium. The following are a few items that will give you a head start.

As mentioned earlier, water quality test kits are very important. Make sure that when you purchase your complete aquarium setup that these are not left out. Test kits that measure pH, hardness and nitrogen compounds are a must. Included in the latter should be tests for ammonia, nitrite and nitrate.

There are some other handy accessories that will help you keep your tank clean. An algal sponge or aquarium cleaner is a sponge attached to a long handle used for scraping down the inside of the tank without having to empty the aquarium out. The sponge will easily scrape off algae, but will not scratch the tank. A magnetic aquarium cleaner is also an effective cleaning tool. This uses two magnets with cleaning surfaces. One magnet is kept outside the tank and the other is controlled on the inside walls of the tank by the outside magnet.

An aquarium vacuum is a must for the beginner. This is usually a hand pump siphon that enables you to extract larger debris from the aquarium floor without having to submerse your hands or use a net.

You will definitely need a fishnet or two. It's better to have several sizes handy, depending on the size of your tank and the size of your fish. Too small a net will be difficult to use to corner a fish, and too large a net will be difficult to maneuver in

the tank. You will use a fishnet more often than you think. It will come in very handy when you need to remove a fish that is ill, dead or aggressive, or when the time has come to clean the tank and remove all the fish.

There are other items you will use during routine aquarium maintenance that you will want to have within arm's reach. Set aside a 5-gallon bucket and a siphon hose of adequate length for use only with your aquarium. This will lessen the need to prepare a clean bucket or hose every time you use one, and it will lessen the likelihood of introducing toxic agents into the

With sufficient swimming space and a clean environment, your fish will thrive. (Schomburgk's Pacu)

aquarium each time you use a different bucket or hose.

Although not an essential piece of equipment, an aquarium backdrop or screen is preferred by many aquarists. The aquarium backdrop is a paper or plastic backing that you place on the exterior back wall of the aquarium. This will conceal tubes, filters, pumps and other fixtures that are usually kept on the back of the tank. Because many tanks are placed against the wall, the backdrop also covers the paint or wallpaper behind the tank. Aquarium backdrops come in a variety of colors, shades, and scenes. Choose one that you find most appealing and that fits the decor of your aquarium.

Before you purchase the decorative components of your tank, take the time to sketch out on paper just how you want your aquarium to look. Include the gravel, plants, decorations and the backdrop when you do so. Keep in mind that fish require shelters as well as swimming space. Therefore, visualize your aquarium with rocks, caves and areas of refuge. Once you have a conceptual design in mind and on paper, setting up your aquarium will be much easier.

SETTING UP THE AQUARIUM

The first step to properly setting up your new aquarium is to assemble all the components in the area where you want the aquarium to be. (Remember to follow the guidelines outlined above when choosing the right location for your aquarium.) Inventory the various pieces of the aquarium and make sure that you are not lacking any essential component.

Successful Setup

Once you are confident that everything is in order, take the following steps to set up your aquarium.

1. Make sure everything is clean. Give the gravel, tank, filter, heater, aquarium decorations, artificial plants and anything else you expect to put in the tank a thorough rinsing with clean, warm water. Residues, dirt and toxic agents can accumulate on your equipment between the time it is manufactured and the time it gets to your home. When it comes to cleaning aquarium decorations like rocks and wood, use a scrubbing brush to remove

dirt. Never use any kind of soap when cleaning your aquarium components; this can cause immediate water quality problems.

2. Place the tank on its stand exactly where you want it to reside. Do not expect to move the tank once it is filled with water. Now it is time to begin assembling the interior of your aquarium. Aquascape your tank beginning with the lowermost layer, the gravel. If you are going to use an undergravel filter, remember to add it before gently pouring the gravel into the tank. Terrace the gravel so that it is higher in the back than in the front of the tank.

3. Add any larger pieces of rock or wood. Remember to follow your plan, making changes where you see fit. Don't attempt to add plants (either real or artificial) or smaller decorations until the water is added to the tank; they may be disrupted by the filling process. Remember to leave spaces for heaters, filters and other equipment.

4. This would be an appropriate time to add the airstones to the

TANK TIPS

The following are some basic points to keep in mind when choosing your aquarium tank.

- Choose the largest tank you can afford and accommodate

- Choose a long rectangular tank rather than a tall one

- Choose glass rather than acrylic

- Make sure there are no gaps in the sealant

aquarium, taking the opportunity to conceal air supply tubing behind larger decorations.

5. Add water to the tank. To avoid disrupting your aquascape, place a clean plate or bowl on the substrate and pour the water onto it. In most households, tap water will be the appropriate water source. If you suspect that your tap water is excessively hard or soft or contains high levels of chloramine, check with your local water company. In these cases, you may need to purchase water or chemically treat your tap water. As a rule, the aquarium aging process combined with filtration will alleviate minor tap water problems.

33

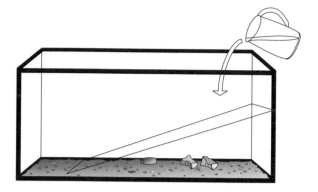

Pour water into the aquarium over a slanted surface so as not to disrupt your aquascape.

34

6. Place the filter and heater in the tank and position them. Prepare the former by following manufacturer instructions regarding filter media before setting it on or in the tank. Position the heater in such a way as to maximize its output. Place it near sources of water circulation like filter outlets or airstones.

7. Place the smaller decorations in the tank, add the thermometer, and fine-tune your aquascape. Add artificial plants according to your plan. If you are going to add live plants, do not do so until the appropriate temperatures suitable for your plants have been attained. It is best to get your tank up and running before buying your live plants. Once added to the tank, live plants may need to be weighted

down until root systems are well established.

8. Fit the hood, making sure that the external components and electrical equipment are properly placed. Add the light on top of the canopy and make sure that it is hooked up correctly.

9. When you are confident that the electrical wiring is safely insulated from sources of water, plug the aquarium units in and turn on the system. Make sure that the heater is properly adjusted; it may take a day or two for the water to reach the right temperature. Check the operation of the filter, air pumps and light.

10. Let the tank water mature before adding any fish.

AQUARIUM MATURATION

When you have completed the above steps you will have a tank filled with water, but you will not have the working, well-balanced, artificial habitat that is an aquarium. To get to this, you need to let the tank mature. Recall that fish require suitable water quality with appropriate levels of water pH and hardness. Your tap water may harbor treatment additives that can harm your fish. In addition, your new tank does not have a well-established nitrogen cycle. Water circulation, temperature regulation and filtration will help your water mature in a relatively short period of time.

The estimated period of water conditioning varies, depending on what kind of setup you have. The new undergravel filter will take between four and six weeks to fully establish itself. Many feel that you should wait a minimum of ten to fourteen days before introducing fish into your aquarium. On the other hand, some fish keepers have added fish to a new tank in as little as one to two days after initial setup. It depends on when your pH and hardness stabilize and how well you have established the nitrogen cycle. There are commercial treatments available that will accelerate the maturation process. If you decide to use one of these, get advice from your local dealer and read the instructions carefully.

It is important to test your water daily to determine when you can add fish to the tank. In general, once pH and hardness have stabilized in

BRINGING YOUR FISH HOME

When you bring a fish home, the pet dealer will put it in a plastic bag with water and enough oxygen for a short trip. Ask to have the plastic bag placed inside a dark opaque bag. Keeping the fish in the dark will help reduce the stress of the trip. You must resist the temptation to take the fish out and admire it. Bringing the fish in and out of the dark can put it in shock. Keep it in the bag until you get home.

two to four days, the next step is to fuel the nitrogen cycle. This can be done by introducing a few very hardy, inexpensive fish, like common goldfish, into the tank. These fish will produce the necessary ammonia that will help establish bacterial colonies that comprise the nitrogen cycle.

Once the fish have been introduced, it is important to continue to monitor ammonia, nitrite and nitrate levels. You may see ammonia and nitrite levels begin to climb rapidly, but the nitrate will remain low. If you have introduced the fish too soon, this situation can result in the poisoning of the fish, a phenomenon known as "new tank syndrome." This means that the bacterial colonies that convert these compounds into the less harmful nitrate are not yet established. In most cases, if you wait a few days before introducing your starter fish, this will not occur.

Gradually, in about one to two weeks, your ammonia levels will stabilize, nitrite will decrease and nitrate will increase. This is a sure sign that it is time to add more fish to your aquarium. Do this slowly, adding a fish or two every few days. Remember to calculate the maximum number of fish that your tank can accommodate and use this number conservatively. Continue to monitor ammonia, nitrite and nitrate levels throughout this period.

If a sudden peak occurs in ammonia and/or nitrite, stop adding fish until that peak diminishes.

ADDING FISH TO THE TANK

When you leave your pet store, you will most likely have your selected fish packed in plastic bags. Make sure that the dealer fills the airspace in the bag with oxygen. Take care not to disturb or shock your fish during transport. Follow these steps when you get home.

1. Float the plastic bag containing your fish in the tank so that the temperature in the bag can

It is important to make sure that your aquarium's water has matured and stabilized before you add the fish.

acclimate to that in the aquarium. Let it sit in the tank for at least ten to fifteen minutes.

2. Open the bag to let some fresh air in and seal it again. To ensure that the fish will not be shocked by the aquarium water, make sure that the temperature of the water in the bag and in the aquarium are within a degree of each other. Add a handful of water from your aquarium to the bag and let it sit for another ten to fifteen minutes.

3. Now you can add the fish to the tank by simply and gently inverting the bag into the tank, letting the fish out.

A Quarantine Tank

In order to evaluate the health of the fish, serious aquarists establish a quarantine tank for new fish to inhabit for the first few days. A quarantine tank is a much smaller and simpler aquarium set up just for quarantine purposes. The quarantine tank needs to be properly filtered and tested routinely, just as the main aquarium. As a beginner, you shouldn't need such a tank if you buy hardy fish from a resputable dealer.

CHAPTER THREE

A Quality Home

You have planned your aquarium, purchased your equipment, set up your tank, established excellent water quality, carefully selected and introduced the fish and fed them well. Now it is time to learn how to maintain the quality of their new home. Aquarium maintenance involves everything from turning the light on and off everyday and feed-

Socoloff's Cichlid

ing the fish to spending time observing the fish. This latter task is often the most enjoyable. Get to know your fish, watch how they interact and make note of any unusual behavior. Closely check the fish for any signs of disease and watch their interactions to see if any are being picked on. If you have live plants, check them to see if any parts of them are brown or dying. If they are, remove these sections at once.

If the conditions in the aquarium are kept constant, the fish are unlikely to become stressed. Rapid fluctuations in water temperature and water quality will cause stress and therefore compromise the health of your fish. You must

monitor the water temperature, making sure that it does not change. Examine the filter, the heater and the airstones to make sure that they are in working order. The filter may be experiencing some blockage, especially if you are using a box filter. The thermostat light in the heater should be working properly. Verify that the air pump and airstones are operating at maximum efficiency. These things should be checked daily and require just a few moments of your time. While you are feeding or simply enjoying your pets, you can perform a routine check of the tank components and the aquarium occupants.

GENERAL MAINTENANCE

Cleaning an aquarium involves an active, conscientious effort on your part. Maintaining a fish tank is not for the lazy at heart. Don't set up a tank if you don't intend to follow through and keep it clean and healthy. All too often, interest wanes after the first few months, and the aquarium ultimately suffers the consequences. Realize that going into this hobby requires a real commitment on your part. Concern must be shown at every step and on every level. Your fishes' lives depend on your attention to detail.

Vacuuming

Vacuuming is one of the most important parts of maintaining your tank. You must prevent the accumulation of mulm or detritus in the gravel. Mulm is the combination of fish wastes, plant fragments and uneaten food that settles on the bottom of the aquarium and decays. If not removed, this organic waste will ultimately break down into nitrites and nitrates via the nitrogen cycle. This in turn will disturb your water chemistry, potentially harming your fish. If detritus is allowed to accumulate to excessive levels, your filter will be clogged and water quality will go downhill fast. If you have an undergravel filter, vacuuming is still very important because too much mulm will clog these filters as well, preventing water flow through the gravel.

Aquarium vacuums are available from your pet dealer. A wide hose is recommended to siphon wastes while you are doing a water change. This in effect accomplishes two goals at once: Vacuuming mulm and removing water from the tank.

39

An industrious bottom-feeder, like this Sailfin Pleco, will help keep the aquarium's rocks, plants and gravel free of debris and algae.

Check the Filter

Assuming you have an external filter or a box filter, it is very important to check the filter media. The top level mat gets dirty quickly and easily, as this is the level that collects the largest pieces of debris. An excessive buildup of detritus in your filter will inhibit flow and ultimately reduce the filter's effectiveness.

Rinse the filter mat under luke-warm water every three or four months until the water is clear. You should probably replace about 50 percent of the media every six months, making sure to reuse about half of the old filter material. You have established a viable working bacterial colony in your filter medium, and you don't want to throw it out and start from the beginning. That's why some of the old media must be retained. One of the most common mistakes is the replacement of the entire filter contents every few months because it looks dirty. Some of that "dirt" is bacteria that's beneficial to the filtering process. For filters that utilize cartridges as media, check with the manufacturer for optimum maintenance and replacement rate.

Algae

What exactly is algae and do all algae cause problems for your tank?

Algae are actually plants that belong to the class known as *Thallophyta*, the same class as fungi. They are relatively simple plants that range in size from the one-celled microscopic types to large seaweeds that grow to over 230 feet. Algae are also very hardy plants that have a tremendous reproductive capacity. They can enter your aquarium as airborne algal spores or can be carried by new plants, snails and tank furnishings from another aquarium.

Most species of algae occur in the waters and, like fish, have adapted to all kinds of water conditions. In your aquarium, they can be found on the surface, suspended in the water or on the surfaces of rocks, gravel and tank decorations.

In low levels, algae can be somewhat beneficial to the aquarium, providing the same benefits as plants. But if algae is present, it will generally grow in excess if the right conditions exist. Excessive algal growth will overrun a tank unless water quality is properly maintained. High nitrate levels and sunlight will promote algal growth. Avoiding these conditions will minimize algae as a tank nuisance.

If you seem to have excessive algal growth, there are several measures you can employ to reduce the presence of algae in the aquarium.

- The introduction of algae eaters like Flying Foxes, Black Mollies and Corydoras catfish will serve to keep algae in check on gravel, rocks and plants.

- Keep the aquarium well planted; nitrates will be consumed by healthy aquarium plants instead of being available for algae.

- Reduce the duration of light from twelve hours to ten hours per day.

- Make sure that all rocks, plants, decorations and gravel going into the tank are free of algae.

- Scrape algae from the aquarium walls with an algae scraper. These are usually either sponges attached

It is important to clean away the surface film of algae and dirt. Here, a magnetized scraper is used.

Beautiful fish will flourish in a clean, well-maintained aquarium environment. (Discus)

42

to a long stick, a razor blade attached to a stick or magnetic scrapers.

- Remove excess nitrates, which will fuel algal growth by carrying out partial water changes in a timely fashion.

Don't become obsessed with algae to the point where you feel that all algae must be removed from the aquarium. It is all but impossible to remove all algae. Expect to live with a little algae in your tank.

Test the Water

When you first set up the aquarium, testing the water every few days is critical to the water maturation process. When you begin to add fish, water chemistry changes radically, and water quality monitoring is critical to the survival of your fish. After this sensitive period of two to four weeks, it is still very important to test your water; you should do so every week for the first two months. This will give you a good understanding of the mechanics of the nitrogen cycle and will indicate to you when the nitrates have reached a level where a water change is needed.

After two months, your tank will certainly be well established and the need to test the water every week will diminish. At this point, a monthly water test will suffice unless you suspect that you might have tank problems. Sudden behavioral changes in your fish, fish disease, fish mortality, excessive algal growth, "smelly" water and cloudy water all warrant an immediate water quality test and possible water change.

Water Changes

Water changes are one of the most important aspects of cleaning and maintaining your tank. A water change is when you literally take out a percentage of the aquarium water and replace it with fresh or distilled water. The amount you change varies with the quality of your tank and with the frequency of water changes. Some experts believe that a 10 percent water change is sufficient every week, while others hold that this volume should be closer to 30 percent. You should start with a water change of 10 to 20 percent every week and raise or lower this amount depending on water quality.

Water changes help to maintain good water quality because you are diluting the amount of nitrogenous compounds like nitrites and nitrates,

harmful gases and other toxic substances each time you change the water. The water you add, which should be pure distilled water if possible, will be more oxygen rich than the water in your tank.

The best way to conduct a water change is to use a siphon and a large bucket. The siphon is basically just a 3- or 4-foot hose or tube that will transfer water from the tank to the bucket.

HOW TO SIPHON

1. Fill the tube completely with water, making sure there is no trapped air anywhere in the tube. Make sure that the siphon is clean and that your hands are clean as well. You can fill the hose at the sink or by submerging it in the aquarium. Only do the latter if your aquarium is large enough to accommodate the hose without spooking the fish. Use your thumbs to block

A water changer can be used to siphon and to refill the tank while maintaining acceptable water conditions.

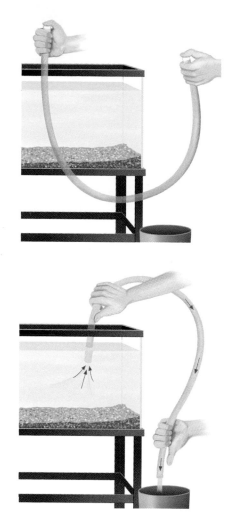

Siphoning:
Step 1

44

Siphoning:
Step 2

bucket end is lower than the aquarium or siphoning will not work. If you filled your siphon in the aquarium, plug one end of the hose tightly, lift it from the aquarium and lower it to the bucket.

3. Release your thumbs and the water will begin to flow rapidly from the aquarium into the bucket.

As mentioned earlier, use the siphon to remove debris from the tank while you are making a water change. When it is time to add water and if distilled water is not available, use tap water that you have allowed to age for one or two days. Either keep a few 1-gallon jugs stored in the house or keep a 5-gallon bucket filled with water for a few days. Make sure that the water you add is close in temperature to that of your aquarium.

There are now devices that can be attached to your tank that will change the water for you on a constant basis. Whether you have chlorinated water or not, your pet store will be able to supply you with one of these water changers. It makes life much easier but requires that you have a faucet constantly

both ends of the siphon to keep the water in and air out.

2. Keeping your thumbs in place, place one end of the hose in the aquarium and aim the other at the bucket. Make sure that the

available somewhere near the aquarium. Water changers are labor-saving devices that make maintenance much easier and life better for your fish.

MAINTENANCE CHECKLIST

Note: A monthly maintenance checklist appears on the convenient tear-out card in the front of this book. You may want to put the checklist on your refrigerator or place it near your aquarium.

Daily

- Feed the fish twice a day.
- Turn the tank lights on and off.
- Check the water temperature.
- Check the heater and make sure the thermostat light is working.
- Make sure the filter(s) are working properly.
- Make sure the aerator is working properly.

Weekly

- Study the fish closely, watching for behavioral changes and signs of disease.

- Change approximately 10 to 20 percent of the aquarium water.
- Add distilled or aged water to compensate for water evaporation.
- Check the filter to see if the top mat needs to be replaced.
- Vacuum the tank thoroughly and attempt to clean up mulm and detritus.
- Test the water for pH, nitrates and softness (first two months).
- Trim and fertilize aquarium plants as needed.

Monthly

- Change 25 percent of the aquarium water.
- Clean the tank's inside glass with an algae scraper.
- Vacuum the tank thoroughly, stirring up the gravel and eliminating mulm.
- Test the water for pH, nitrates and softness.
- Rinse any tank decorations that suffer from dirt buildup.
- Trim and fertilize plants; replace plants if necessary.

45

Quarterly

- Change 50 percent of the water; replace with distilled or aged water.

- Replace airstones.

- Rinse filter materials completely and replace some if necessary.

- Clean the inside aquarium glass with an algae scraper.

- Vacuum the tank thoroughly, stirring up the gravel and eliminating mulm.

- Trim and fertilize plants as needed; replace if necessary.

- Test the water for pH, nitrates and softness.

- Rinse any tank decorations that suffer from dirt buildup.

Yearly

- Strip down the filter; replace at least 50 percent of the media with new mat and charcoal.

- Replace the airstones.

- Wash the gravel entirely.

- Clean the inside of the tank thoroughly.

- Restart the aquarium all over again, but save some of the original aquarium water to help condition the tank.

CHAPTER FOUR

Freshwater Fish Families

You are most likely to have fresh-water tropical fish in your new aquarium. Although most are now bred in captivity for the aquarium trade, in their natural habitats they are found throughout the world. The diversity of these fish is amazing and can be daunting. In order to make these fish easier to identify, scientists have classified them into different groups.

A particular species has a common name, which can differ depending on the region or the language. However, a species also has a scientific name that is used to identify that species in all languages. The scientific name of a species is based in Latin and is in two parts, the genus and the species. For example,

Red Rasbora

the scientific name of the Neon Tetra is *Paracheirodon innesi* and the Cardinal Tetra's is *Paracheirodon axelrodi*. The first name refers to the genus, or grouping of very similar species, to which both species belong. If you look at these fish, you can see that they are extremely similar. The second name refers only to that species and no other. Similar genera (plural for genus) are classified into families.

In general, most experts prefer to combine freshwater aquarium fish families into two major groups based on their reproductive biology: livebearers and egglayers. The major families of each group follow. Families that have similar characteristics have been grouped together. By no means is this a complete list of tropical freshwater fish families, only those you are most likely to encounter. When a single species has additional varieties or strains, the varieties are a result of selective breeding of that species for certain characteristics and the establishment of a new variety (not a new species). For example, the common goldfish, *Carassius auratus,* has been selectively bred to over 125 recognized varieties.

LIVEBEARERS

The livebearers include four major families (*Anablepidae, Goodeidae, Hemirhamphidae* and *Poeciliidae*) that are kept in captivity. These are the common aquarium fish known as guppies, mollies, platys and

swordtails, as well as the various breeds and strains of each. These are especially hardy fish that breed readily in captivity. The males of these families are easily recognizable by their possession of a gonopudium. This modified pelvic fin is used by the male during mating with the female.

EGGLAYERS

Barbs and Rasboras

These fish belong to the closely related families *Cyprinidae* and *Cobitidae,* which contain over 1,300 species of fish. Loaches, very popular aquarium fish, fall into the latter group. Examples of these fish include the Tiger Barb from Indonesia, the Zebra Danio from India and the Clown Loach from India. The Red-tailed Shark, which is not a shark but actually a rasbora, is also a member of this family; it originates in Thailand.

Catfish

There are fifteen families and 2,000 species of catfish that contribute to the aquarium trade. The so-called armored catfish (*Loricariidae, Callichthyidae*), include the popular "plecostomus" fish and other algae eaters found in home aquariums. This group also includes the 140 species of Corydoras catfish with their large heads and short bodies. These South American catfish are known for their propensity to feed on the substrate, thereby cleaning the tank bottom. Other families include the banjo catfish, the naked catfish, the glass catfish and the pim catfish. Most of these fish are peaceful and easily adapt to a community tank.

Characins

The Characins contain thirteen families of fish more commonly known as the tetras. There are over 1,300 species of tetras originating mostly in South America, but also originating in Africa. Common characteristics of this group include the possession of a toothed jaw and an adipose fin or second dorsal fin. In many species, males can be distinguished from females by the possession of hooklike spines on the anal fin or projecting from the base of the tail. These fish are generally school forming in their natural habitat. Two of the most popular characins with very different

dispositions are the Neon Tetra and the Red-bellied Piranha. A small school of the former is an attractive addition to the aquarium, but the latter belongs in a single species tank. Overall, most members of this group are peaceful and make excellent additions to the community aquarium.

Cichlids

The family *Cichlidae* contains over 900 species of fish originating from Central and South America, parts of the Caribbean, southern India and across Africa. Cichlids inhabit a wide range of habitats throughout these areas including salt water and high temperature water (104°F). Most cichlids are small to medium-size with a single dorsal fin that is usually composed of hard and soft rays. Some species, like the freshwater angelfish, are compressed laterally and have long ornate fins. Temperament in this group ranges from pugnacious and intolerant to very peaceful. Care should be taken when selecting cichlids for the community aquarium. Common cichlids include the Jack Dempsey, oscar, angelfish and discus. A common behavior among many African lake

49

Cichlids are a family of egglaying fish in which temperament can vary widely, depending upon the species. (Freiberg's Peacock Cichlid)

cichlids is mouthbrooding, during which the female will take her fertilized eggs into her mouth until they hatch. Often the fry will return to her mouth for shelter. Cichlids can be extremely territorial and some mate for life.

Killifish

Killifish belong primarily to two families, the *Aplocheilidae* and the *Cyprinodontidae*. They are very diverse fish with more than 450 species spanning all the continents with the exceptions of Australia and Antarctica. Killifish have permeated saltwater, brackish and freshwater habitats throughout their range. Distinctive rounded scales and a lateral line system only on the area

around the head are characteristic features of this group. Some of the more common members of this group include the lyretails, rivulus and lampeyes.

Labyrinth Fish

This group of four families is so-named for the special organ inside their head called the labyrinth. This organ allows the fish to breathe in air at the surface. The inhaled air is pressed into the labyrinth and the oxygen is drawn from it there. This enables these fish to live and survive in oxygen-depleted waters. Many of these fish come from Thailand, Indonesia, Cambodia and Malaysia. The most popular of the labyrinth fish belong to the family *Belontiidae*, which includes the Gouramis, Paradise Fish and Bettas. The Paradise Fish is extremely hardy, but becomes very territorial in an aquarium as an adult. The Betta is better known as the Siamese Fighting Fish, so-named because the males fight and tear their finnage to shreds. Although sometimes displayed in very small fish bowls, these fish should not be kept in less than a liter of water; they are very sensitive to temperature changes. The Gouramis are very popular additions to the community tank; they are peaceful fish with ornate fins and prefer heavy vegetation. The only member

of the family *Helostomatiidae* maintained in captivity is the popular Kissing Fish. Native to Thailand, these fish are actually displaying aggression when "kissing" another member of the species.

Rainbowfish

The group known as rainbowfish is comprised of three families mostly originating from New Guinea and eastern Australia. Members of this group are peaceful, active schooling fish with oval, laterally compressed bodies. A common member of this group is the Splendid Rainbow.

Labyrinth fish, like this Siamese Fighting Fish, have a special organ inside their heads that allows them to breathe in air at the water's surface.

Knifefish

The unique group of knifefish is comprised of four families. The speckled knifefish (*Apteronotidae*), the banded knifefish (*Gymnotidae*) and the American knifefish (*Rhamphichthyidae*) are found in Central and South America. The fourth family, *Notopteridae*, comes from the fresh waters of Africa and Asia. These fish are so-named for their laterally compressed, blade-shaped tapered body form. Most species are nocturnal and peaceful, but they should be kept with fish of similar size. Some of the Notopterid knifefish, however, are aggressive and are best kept alone.

Mormyrids

Commonly known as the elephant-nose fish, species of the family *Mormyridae* have mouths extended like an elephant's trunk. Found in Africa, these fish use this modified mandible as a sensory organ. They also possess an organ near their tail that generates weak electric signals. When an elephantnose becomes nervous, its electric pulse rate increases. The continuous pulsing of the electric organ can disturb other aquarium fish as well as other elephantnose fish.

OTHER POPULAR FISH

There are at least forty families of fish kept in aquariums that are not covered above. They are so diverse in form and behavior that discussion of each is not possible. Consult one of the fish encyclopedias listed in the bibliography (chapter 9) for more information on the wide variety of fish families. These references not only describe each species available to the aquarist, but list the specific aquarium requirements of each species. Groups of families reviewed above are those most commonly seen in pet stores.

CHAPTER FIVE

Choosing the Right Fish

Day's Spinetail Gourami

Throughout this book, your aquarium has been referred to as a community tank. The community tank contains different species of compatible fish, while the species tank contains only a single species of fish. The beginner is usually wise to begin with a community tank; the species tank concept is best for those who want to maintain fish that require special tank conditions or that are extremely aggressive.

THE BEST AQUARIUM FISH FOR BEGINNERS

There are a wide variety of fish that are well-suited for the community aquarium. It is important to balance the types of fish in your tank. You will recall that species of fish have adapted to varying lifestyles and different habitats. There are fish that live in the topwater, the midwater and on the bottom. In the community tank, you want to re-create this kind of environment by having fish spread throughout the tank on every level.

In addition, many species of fish school by nature. This behavior can be a very attractive addition to the community tank. Schooling fish should never be kept alone but rather in a group of at least five or six individuals.

As mentioned earlier in the general overview, some fish tend to be aggressive. These should be avoided by the beginner because a single antagonistic fish in a community tank can wreak havoc on the other species.

Another aspect the novice will sometimes overlook is the maximum size of a particular species. A fish will grow continuously throughout its life. Some species grow faster than others. You don't want to put a fish in your tank that will attain a length of 12 inches in less than a year. This will not only disrupt your aquarium capacity, but the larger fish will undoubtedly dominate the

tank. Some species are very compatible with other species when they are juveniles but become solitary and aggressive as adults. These fish do not belong in the peaceful community tank.

When your tank is fully established, the water chemistry is balanced and you are ready to stock your aquarium, you should have a game plan in mind. Don't blindly go to your pet dealer and look for fish to fill your tank. This can result in fish incompatibility. Instead, decide on the kind of fish you want to start with beforehand. Use some of the following suggestions and consult some of the fish encyclopedias listed in chapter 9, "Recommended Reading." In other words, establish a good list of potential fish that you want to introduce into your aquarium. Remember to choose a variety of species that will live throughout the water column from the top to the bottom.

Be selective when you get to the pet store. Buy fish only from clean aquariums with clear water, clean panes and no dead fish in the tank. Make sure that the fish you want appears to be healthy. If the fish has any cuts, scrapes or fin problems, don't buy it. Watch for possible symptoms of disease such as white granular spots, cottony white patches, frayed fins or dull skin. Watch the behavior of the fish. Healthy fish swim in a lively manner and are not shy.

Most fish keepers agree that it is important to introduce your fish to the aquarium in batches, buying fish in lots every ten to fourteen days. This is important for the newly established aquarium. This allows fish to acclimate to each other and prevents aggressive behavior toward a single fish when it is introduced.

The following is a list of species that are particularly easy to care for. They are well suited for the beginner's community tank where pH ranges from 6.5 to 7.5 and temperature is maintained between 75° and 79°F. These recommendations are arranged according to the part of your tank that they are most likely to inhabit: topwater, midwater and bottom.

Topwater Fish

The topwater fish are not restricted to the upper levels of the tank, but are more likely to be seen there. For these species, feeding and spawning, in particular, occur at or near the surface of the aquarium.

GUPPY *(Poecilia reticulata)*
Family: *Poeciliidae*
Distribution: Central America to Brazil
Size: Males $1^{1}/_{2}$ inches, females $2^{1}/_{2}$ inches
Food: Omnivorous
Temperature: 64° to 81°F

This species is a definite favorite among beginners because it is a very hardy fish that gives birth to live young every month. The male is very colorful with ornate finnage and a gonopodium; females are dull in coloration. Selective breeding has resulted in the production of over 100 varieties. These fish are vigorous swimmers and prefer to live in small groups of four to six members. Provide plenty of cover and floating plants, and you may be able to successfully raise the fry.

Guppy.

Green Swordtail.

GREEN SWORDTAIL
(Xiphophorus helleri)
Family: *Poeciliidae*
Distribution: Central America
Size: Males 4 inches, females 4¹/₂ inches
Food: Omnivorous
Temperature: 68° to 79°F

The Green Swordtail is a popular community fish because it breeds readily in captivity. The males possess a long swordlike extension on the lower part of their tail that develops as they mature (hence the species' common name). The males can be temperamental and will harass the females, so it is best to have the females outnumber the males; males will quarrel with each other as well. These fish breed every twenty-eight days at 74°F. Like the guppy, dense vegetation will provide cover for developing fry. Another benefit of this species is its tendency to consume algae.

BLACK MOLLY
(Poecilia sphenops)
Family: *Poeciliidae*
Distribution: Mexico to Colombia
Size: 2¹/₂ inches
Food: Omnivorous
Temperature: 64° to 82°F

The Black Molly is actually a hybrid of the original variety, the Mexican Molly. The many varieties prefer temperatures on the upper end of the range. Other varieties include the green, marbled, albino and lyretail mollies. This species is another livebearer that is gentle and basically

Black Sailfin Molly.

a vegetable eater. Like the swordtail, the molly will consume aquarium algae, keeping it in check. This species is lively and prefers residing in small groups of four to six members. Although not as hardy as other livebearers, the molly will prosper if aquarium conditions are kept constant.

PLATY *(Xiphophorus maculatus)*

Family: Poeciliidae
Distribution: Mexico and Guatemala to Honduras
Size: Males 4 inches, females 4$^1/_2$ inches
Food: Omnivorous
Temperature: 72° to 79°F

The platy belongs to the same genus as the swordtail and is therefore a very close relative. Some consider it to be the ideal community fish. As with most livebearers, many color

Platy.

varieties have been commercially bred for the home aquarium. Plenty of cover in dense vegetation will lead to successful breeding and the survival of the fry in a community tank. The platy consumes algae and prefers to live in small groups of five to seven fish. A very similar species, the Variable Platy (*Xiphophorus variatus*) is equally as hardy and well suited for the community tank.

Zebra Danio.

ZEBRA DANIO *(Brachydanio rerio)*

Family: *Cyprinidae*
Distribution: India
Size: 2$^1/_2$ inches
Food: Omnivorous
Temperature: 64° to 75°F

The torpedo-shaped danios are very active schooling fish that should be kept in groups of at least seven or eight individuals. This egglaying cyprinid has been commercially bred to create both albino and long-finned strains. Males are generally slimmer than females and usually remain loyal to one female once they have spawned. This species likes to spend time at the surface where it is open and bright. A similar species is the Pearl Danio (*Brachydano albolineatus*).

WHITE CLOUD MOUNTAIN MINNOW *(Tanichthys albonubes)*

Family: *Cyprinidae*
Distribution: Southern China
Size: 1¹/₂ inches
Food: Omnivorous
Temperature: 64° to 72°F

This very undemanding, active cyprinid fish should be kept in a group of eight or more members. Males are slimmer and have more intense coloration than females. However, note that these peaceful

White Cloud Mountain Minnow.

fish prefer cooler water and should only be kept in temperatures less than 72°F.

Silver Hatchetfish.

COMMON HATCHETFISH *(Gasteropelecus sternicia)*

Family: *Gasteropelecidae*
Distribution: Brazil, Guyana, Surinam
Size: 2¹/₂ inches
Food: Carnivorous
Temperature: 73° to 79°F

This surface dweller, and its close relative the Marbled Hatchetfish (*Carnegiella strigata*), are characins that need to be kept in schools of at least six fish. The unusually deep body of these species makes them an interesting addition to any community aquarium. All hatchets are excellent jumpers, so be sure to keep the hood in place on the tank. A few floating plants will provide adequate cover for these gentle fish.

SIAMESE FIGHTING FISH
(Betta splendens)

Family: *Belontiidae*
Distribution: Cambodia, Thailand
Size: 3 inches
Food: Carnivorous
Temperature: 75° to 84°F

This beautiful labyrinth fish is a popular addition to the community aquarium. Selective breeding over the years has enhanced the brilliant ornate finnage of the males. However, only one male may be kept per aquarium, otherwise vicious fighting will occur; duels between males can result in death. Males are generally peaceful with other species unless they have similar fin veils. The smaller, shorter-finned females are more drab but may be kept together in a community tank. This egglaying species builds a bubble nest at the surface of the aquarium where the eggs are guarded by the males.

Midwater Fish

Many of the midwater swimmers belong to the groups of fish referred to as the cyprinids and the characins; most do best in schools of eight or more individuals. With this in mind, the beginner should

consider only one or two species of schooling midwater fish.

Siamese Fighting Fish.

59

ROSY BARB *(Barbus conchonius)*

Family: *Cyprinidae*
Distribution: Northern India
Size: 3 inches
Food: Omnivorous
Temperature: 64° to 72°F

Barbs get their name from the short threadlike barbels that act as sensory organs on either side of their mouths and sometimes on their lips. Their vigor and agility in the mid-waters of the tank contribute greatly to the vitality of the aquarium. Many barbs, however, can cause harm to smaller fish and fish with

Rosy Barb.

ornate veil-like fins. The Rosy Barb is a very peaceful species that adapts well to a community aquarium. However, it prefers cooler water than other community fish and is most colorful in these conditions. A related species, the Tiger Barb (*Barbus tetrazona*) has a bit wilder disposition when introduced singly or as a pair. This fish will wreak havoc among other occupants, nipping fins and harassing them. However, if kept in schools of eight or more members, they establish a hierarchy and generally leave other fish alone. It is recommended that schools contain both the more colorful males and the heavier females. This Indonesian species prefers warmer water in the range of 68° to 79°F. The Ruby Barb (*Barbus nigrofasciatus*) of Sri Lanka also prefers warmer water and, when in the company of other barbs, is a peaceful addition to the community tank.

RED RASBORA *(Rasbora heteromorpha)*

Family: *Cyprinidae*
Distribution: Southeast Asia
Size: 2 inches
Food: Omnivorous
Temperature: 72° to 77°F

This popular species is another schooling cyprinid that requires a group of eight or more fish to be at its best. Because of its size, it should be kept with other equally small and peaceful species. Males are distinguishable from females by a slightly rounded edge at the bottom of the black body marking. The Red Rasbora is deeper bodied than its close relative, the Red-striped Rasbora (*Rasbora pauciperforata*), which is streamlined in shape. This species gets about 1 inch larger than the Red Rasbora, has similar temperature preferences and is ideal for the community aquarium when

Red Rasbora.

maintained in groups of eight or more individuals. Egglaying species of rasboras are not as easy to breed as the barbs, but they are extremely peaceful.

NEON TETRA *(Paracheirodon innes)*

Family: *Characidae*
Distribution: Peru
Size: 1¹/₂ inches
Food: Omnivorous
Temperature: 68° to 79°F

Capable of tolerating a wide range of temperatures, this characin is considered by many to be the most popular of all aquarium fish. Like other midwater fish, the Neon Tetra should be kept in a school of six or more individuals. The iridescent coloration of this fish will glow if the tank is properly lighted. Related species, including the Cardinal Tetra (*Paracheirodon axelrodi*) and the Glowlight Tetra (*Hemmigrammus erythrozonus*), are also peaceful shoaling (schooling) fish that contribute greatly to a community tank. The Black Neon Tetra (*Hyphessobrycon herbertazelrodi*) has a stouter body than the Neon Tetra and makes an ideal community fish as well. In all these species of tetra, the males are generally slimmer than the females.

Neon Tetra.

ANGELFISH *(Pterophyllum scalare)*

Family: *Cichlidae*
Distribution: Central Amazon to Peru, Ecuador
Size: 6 inches
Food: Omnivorous
Temperature: 75° to 82°F

The unique beauty of these fish is very appealing to the beginner, but you must have a well-established aquarium with constant water conditions. They cannot tolerate extreme fluctuations in water quality and temperature. Once you have established your aquarium and water quality remains constant, the introduction of this species is justified. These are placid fish that require tall decorations (like plants) among which they will stay quietly. They are best kept in small groups of four to six members with other even-tempered fish like Neon

Angelfish.

Tetras and Black Mollies. The angelfish is one of the few cichlids that has a somewhat peaceful disposition. However, this species can get up to 6 inches long, and once it attains this size, it will eat smaller fish. The many varieties of angelfish come in a wide range of patterns and colors.

BLUE GOURAMI
(Trichogaster trichopterus)

Family: *Belontiidae*
Distribution: Southeast Asia to Indo-Australian Islands
Size: 4 inches
Food: Omnivorous
Temperature: 72° to 82°F

The Blue Gourami and its relatives, the Dwarf Gourami (*Colisa lalia*),

the Snakeskin Gourami (*Trichogaster pectoralis*) and the Pearl Gourami (*Trichogaster leeri*), are peaceful labyrinth fish that do not need to be kept in groups but do quite well in pairs. Their elaborate finnage and various color forms warrant that care be taken not to include them with fin nippers like Tiger Barbs. Although listed here as midwater fish, the gouramis will swim among the bottom decorations and make frequent excursions to the surface. These egglayers build bubble nests during spawning like other labyrinth fish. The Paradise Fish (*Macropodu opercularis*) closely resembles the gouramis and is also a very hardy labyrinth fish that can tolerate temperatures as low as 61°F. However, this species may cause trouble, annoying other community species if they are very slow; adult males will frequently fight.

Blue Gourami.

Glass Catfish.

GLASS CATFISH
(Kryptopeterus bichirrhis)
Family: *Siluridae*
Distribution: Eastern India and Southeast Asia
Size: 4 inches
Food: Carnivorous
Temperature: 72° to 79°F

This species is one of the few aquarium catfish that does not inhabit the tank bottom. Like other midwater fish, this shoaling species should be placed with at least four of its peers. The Glass Catfish has a transparent body. Although sometimes difficult to acclimate to the aquarium, this hardy fish is a worthwhile addition to the community tank.

Bottom Fish

These fish generally belong to the catfish group, but there are other species that prefer to stay on or near the bottom. The bottom fish are usually tank cleaners, eating bottom detritus and algae. Therefore, no aquarium would be complete without a few.

CORYDORAS CATFISH
(Corydoras species*)*
Family: *Callichthyidae*
Distribution: South America
Size: 1¹/₂ to 2¹/₂ inches
Food: Omnivorous
Temperature: 72° to 79°F

The Corydoras catfish are a genus of fish that are very similar to one another and come in many varieties. They are generally very hardy fish that feed on the substrate with their whiskerlike barbels. Popular species include the Bronze Corydoras (*Corydoras aeneus*), the Arched Corydoras (*Corydoras arcuatus*), Axelrod's Corydoras (*Corydoras*

63

Corydoras undulatus.

axelrodi), the Leopard Corydoras (*Corydoras julii*) and the Dusky Corydoras (*Corydoras septentrionalis*). These fish have a flat bottom so they can stay close to the substrate. They have an adipose fin and armored bony plates rather than scales. They tend to be nocturnal, going about their cleaning business at night. During the day, they like to find a quiet place to hide. They like to live with others of their species, so keep three to five fish together. Don't depend on the substrate to feed these fish; their diets should be augmented with other foods.

FLYING FOX *(Epalzeorhynchus kallopterus)*

Family: *Cyprinidae*
Distribution: Borneo, Indonesia, Thailand, India
Size: 6 inches
Food: Omnivorous
Temperature: 75° to 79°F

Flying Fox.

The Flying Fox is not strictly a bottom species because it will also rest on the leaves of broad-leaved plants or graze algae on large, flat stones. This species is a loner, so it does not require the company of others of its kind, although several can be kept in an aquarium if ample space is provided for each to establish a territory.

Clown Loach.

CLOWN LOACH *(Botia macracanthus)*

Family: *Cobitidae*
Distribution: Borneo, India
Size: 6 inches
Food: Omnivorous
Temperature: 77° to 86°F

This uniquely colorful species of loach is an excellent addition to any community tank. It has barbels like the catfish and the same bottom cleaning propensity. It is recommended that you keep several young as a school, but only one mature adult in your aquarium.

Red-tailed Shark.

RED-TAILED SHARK
(Epalzeorhynchus bicolor*)*

Family: *Cyprinidae*
Distribution: Thailand
Size: 4¹/₂ inches
Food: Omnivorous
Temperature: 72° to 79°F

This species of tropical fish can be aggressive toward other tank fish, and one should be thoughtful before obtaining a Red-tailed Shark. It is, however, a very popular community tank fish that is carried by many pet dealers. It is best to keep a solitary individual in your tank because these fish occupy territories that they will defend against members of their own species. Put them together only with fast small fish or with easy-going larger fish.

CLOWN PLECOSTOMUS
(Peckoltia arenaria)

Family: *Loricariidae*
Distribution: Peru

Size: 4¹/₂ inches
Food: Herbivorous
Temperature: 72° to 80°F

It would be difficult to cover the bottom fish without including one of the species of plecostomus. These fish are famous for their "window cleaning" abilities. This species is one of the smaller suckermouthed catfish that is ideally suited for the community tank. Others will attain lengths in excess of 10 inches and are not well suited for the beginner. This species has been known to be aggressive to its own kind, so it is best to keep only one in your aquarium. Plenty of cover and caves should be provided.

Clown Plecostomus.

FISH FOR BEGINNERS TO AVOID

There are many species of fish that are not well suited to the beginner's

65

aquarium for a number of reasons. Some may be highly sensitive to fluctuating water quality conditions characteristic of the new aquarium. Others may require special water conditions like softer water or brackish water. The new aquarist should not try to provide this type of habitat without acquiring some experience. Finally, there are a number of species that are not socially compatible with the peaceful community tank. This group includes large carnivorous fish that eat smaller fish, territorial fish that do not tolerate trespassing and mature fish that display aggression and combative behavior during spawning or prespawning periods.

Many of these species are offered by pet stores and may even be promoted by dealers because the juveniles are considered "harmless." Don't be fooled by this argument— these fish grow fast and develop aggressive attitudes early in life. The small flake-eating baby will become a neon-eating carnivore in a matter of months.

Avoid buying fish that require special water conditions. These fish may live for days or weeks in your tank, but chronic stress will set in, the fish's immune response will fail and the fish will ultimately die from disease.

The following is a brief description of those species that you should refrain from introducing into your community aquarium. As you will notice, many of these fish are cichlids.

GREEN DISCUS
(Symphysodon aequifasciatus)
Family: *Cichlidae*
Distribution: Amazon
Size: 6 inches
Food: Carnivorous
Temperature: 79° to 86°F

This very peaceful fish would be a visually attractive addition to the

Green Discus (with fry).

community tank. However, it is best kept in a species aquarium because it requires soft acidic water and becomes territorial when breeding.

Oscar.

OSCAR *(Astronotus ocellatus)*

Family: *Cichlidae*
Distribution: South America
Size: 13 inches
Food: Carnivorous
Temperature: 72° to 77°F

When they are young, these undemanding fish are a favorite among aquarists. However, they rapidly grow to a large size and require small fish or meaty food to satisfy their hefty appetites; goldfish are a common food for domesticated oscars. They can, however, tolerate a wide range of water quality parameters and in that regard are easy to maintain.

RED DEVIL *(Amphilophus labiatus)*

Family: *Cichlidae*
Distribution: Central America
Size: 10 inches
Food: Omnivorous
Temperature: 75° to 79°F

As the name implies, this cichlid is an aggressive territorial fish that will eat anything and everything. This species can be mixed only with species that can take care of themselves.

Red Devil.

JEWEL CICHLID *(Hemichromis bimaculatus)*

Family: *Cichlidae*
Distribution: Central Liberia to Southern Guinea
Size: 6 inches
Food: Omnivorous
Temperature: 70° to 73°F

The Jewel Cichlid is noted for its extremely aggressive behavior when

67

Jewel Cichlid.

breeding. This belligerent fish will establish a territory and aggressively protect it.

JACK DEMPSEY *(Nandopsis octofasciatus)*

Family: *Cichlidae*
Distribution: Central America
Size: 8 inches
Food: Omnivorous
Temperature: 72° to 77°F

This is yet another member of the cichlid family that is intolerant of other species. The Jack Dempsey

Jack Dempsey Cichlid.

belongs in a species aquarium, otherwise it will incessantly harass other species.

RUNNY-NOSE TETRA *(Hemigrammus bleheri)*

Family: *Charicidae*
Distribution: Colombia, Brazil
Size: 2 inches
Food: Omnivorous
Temperature: 72° to 79°F

This species of tetra is highly sensitive to water quality conditions. Any buildup of nitrates will cause chronic stress and endanger the fish.

Runny-nose Tetra.

TINFOIL BARB *(Barbus schwanefeldi)*

Family: *Cyprinidae*
Distribution: Southeast Asia
Size: 14 inches
Food: Omnivorous
Temperature: 72° to 77°F

Tinfoil Barb.

Although they are commonly offered in pet stores for the community tank, these fish are very active and grow far too large for the average aquarium. They require a lot of space, are best kept in schools and have a tendency to dig up the substrate.

SUCKING LOACH
(Gyrinocheilus aymonieri)
Family: *Gyrinocheilidae*
Distribution: India, Thailand
Size: 11 inches

Sucking Loach.

Food: Herbivorous
Temperature: 77° to 82°F

Like most loaches, this species is an algae eater. However, Sucking Loaches can get aggressive toward their tank mates and become territorial as they get larger. Their large size also precludes inclusion in the community tank.

Red Snakehead.

RED SNAKEHEAD *(Channa micropeltes)*
Family: *Channidae*
Distribution: India, Burma, Thailand, Vietnam, Malaysia
Size: 39 inches
Food: Carnivorous
Temperature: 77° to 82°F

This large carnivore requires warm temperatures and small live fish to feed on. Although juveniles are considered "cute," they grow rapidly and will consume the community.

Mudskipper.

MUDSKIPPER *(Periophthalmus barbarus)*

Family: *Gobiidae*
Distribution: Africa, Southeast Asia, Australia
Size: 6 inches
Food: Carnivorous
Temperature: 77° to 86°F

This fish is becoming increasingly popular in the aquarium trade. However, it requires brackish water, which it needs to leave periodically. Its territorial nature can also pose a problem in a community tank.

CLOWN KNIFEFISH *(Notopterus chitala)*

Family: *Notopteridae*
Distribution: Southeast Asia

Size: 39 inches
Food: Omnivorous
Temperature: 75° to 82°F

The knifefish in general grows too large for the average community aquarium. This species and its relatives can be extremely aggressive and are best kept alone or with other large fish.

Clown Knifefish.

AROWANA *(Osteoglossum bicirrhosum)*

Family: *Osteoglossidae*
Distribution: Amazon
Size: 47 inches
Food: Carnivorous
Temperature: 75° to 82°F

The Arowana is an elegant fish that enchants the novice as well as the

Arowana.

expert aquarist. However, its large size and predatory nature exclude it from the community aquarium.

As you develop your talents as an aquarist, you will expand your capabilities and be able to keep some of the more sensitive species of fish.

You may even want to establish an aquarium of "compatible" aggressive species or a species tank. However, you should start off with fish that are easier to keep—you will have more success and more fun with your aquarium.

CHAPTER SIX

Fish Nutrition

FEEDING STRATEGIES

There are many considerations when it comes to providing food for your fish. In their natural habitat, fish have developed various feeding strategies to optimize their ability to obtain nourishment. With all the different kinds of fish and habitats, you can imagine the many types of feeding strategies that exist, but there are some similarities among them. Fish can be divided into general groups based on the type of feeding strategy they use.

Carnivores

Carnivore fish are primarily predators that, in nature, feed on smaller fish or larger fish that they

Spotted Puffer

incapacitate. When kept in the aquarium, many of these species have been successfully fed dead food and commercially prepared pellets and flakes. Pieces of fish, shrimp and even bits of meat will be taken by the carnivore, but some species will simply not accept anything but live food. Guppies and goldfish are commonly offered to these predators. None of the recommended community fish outlined in chapter 5 require such measures.

Herbivores

Herbivore fish feed on vegetative matter—plants. This can be a problem if you intend to keep live plants in your aquarium with herbivorous fish. However, if you feed these fish correctly, they will not wreak havoc on your plant community. Fish that require a diet of this nature will consume commercially prepared vegetable flakes. Their diet should be augmented with household vegetables including peas, lettuce, potatoes, beans and cauliflower. Aquarium algae will also attract the herbivore.

Insectivores

Fish with this kind of diet feed on aquatic and terrestrial invertebrates.

FEEDING STRATEGIES

You can divide fish into three groups based on the kind of feeding strategy they use: carnivores, herbivores and omnivores. Carnivores eat only other fish and live food. Piranhas, for example, eat only other fish or animals. Herbivores eat only vegetable matter. They will eat flake foods and other types of plant matter, including the plants in your tank. Angelfish are excellent examples of herbivores. Most of the fish listed in this book are omnivores. They will eat flakes, live foods and bits of table food. Basically, they will eat almost anything. They are clearly the easiest group to feed and are thus the most highly recommended for the beginning aquarist.

As you would expect, these fish readily accept commercially prepared flakes and pellets, but you should also include a variety of invertebrates on top of these foods. Frozen brine shrimp and bloodworms are good examples of what you can feed insectivores.

Omnivores

Omnivore fish feed on a variety of foods and have no specific dietary preferences. You have probably noticed that most of the

73

recommended species outlined in chapter 5 are omnivorous. The beginning aquarist should not have to worry about special feeding strategies when setting up a tank for the first time. These fish will accept commercially prepared flake and pellet foods, but providing a good variety of foods is necessary to meet all their dietary requirements.

FOOD CATEGORIES

There are many different types of food for your tropical freshwater fish. Insectivores will eat flake food, red worms, white worms, earthworms, tubifex, brine shrimp, mosquito larvae and fruit flies. Carnivores will consume almost any kind of seafood—crab, lobster,

oysters and clams. For herbivores, canned vegetables like beans, fresh spinach, broccoli and cauliflower work well. The omnivore will eat all these foods.

There are basically four different categories of food: Flakes or dried foods, live foods, frozen or freeze-dried foods and household foods. Of these, those that can be most harmful to your fish are the live foods, which can carry diseases or parasites that are dangerous to your fish.

Flakes or Dried Foods

Commercially prepared foods contain the three basic requirements of proteins, fats and carbohydrates. They are also supplemented with vitamins and minerals. These foods come in many varieties, depending on the preferred diet, size and feeding behavior of the fish. Flakes, tablets, pellets and crumb forms are available, each appropriate for different types of fish. For example, larger predatory fish should be fed pellets as opposed to flakes because they prefer to consume a large quantity. Fish that feed on the bottom may not venture to the surface for flakes, so they must be fed pellets or tablets that will sink.

A varied diet is important in the maintenance of active, healthy and colorful fish. (Red-tailed Killifish)

All of the community fish discussed in this book will survive on flake foods. However, if you want active, colorful, healthy fish, you should vary their diets. Use flakes as a staple, and make every effort to substitute other foods several times a week.

Live Foods

Live food is an excellent source of nutrition for your fish. Obtain live foods from your pet store, because those collected from a pond or lake may carry diseases that will affect your fish. In any event, this is a great degree easier and safer than collecting live foods yourself.

The only two live foods that generally do not run the risk of carrying a disease are earthworms and brine shrimp. These are easily obtained and will provide an excellent addition to your fish's diet.

BRINE SHRIMP

The brine shrimp (*Artemia salina*) in your local pet store probably originated in the Great Salt Lake area. This is one of the best sources of nutrition available for fish of any type. Of all the live food available, brine shrimp are the safest because

they do not carry diseases. An additional advantage of brine shrimp is that you can raise them yourself. Simply buy a packet of eggs and follow the instructions.

EARTHWORMS

These backyard occupants are rich in protein and a readily available dietary change for your fish. You can either search for them after rain showers on lawns, around pools and lakes, under stones or you can cultivate them in your backyard.

Make sure that no pesticides or weed killers were used in the area where you are cultivating or collecting your earthworms. Such chemicals will assuredly cause harm to your fish.

TUBIFEX

Tubifex are long, thin red worms, also known as sludgeworms, that live in mud and are available from dealers. These live worms are an excellent addition to your fish's diet. Before feeding them to your fish, you must rinse them thoroughly in gently running water for at least one hour. If possible, rinse them for two additional hours. Tubifex require a lot of work and are very risky because their habitat makes them

HOUSEHOLD FOODS
FOR YOUR FISH

Frozen (serve thawed): clams, oysters, lobster, crabmeat, shrimp, fish, mussels

Canned: the same as frozen, plus beans and peas

Raw: the same as frozen, plus ground beef, spinach, lettuce

Cooked: potato, beans, peas, egg yolk, broccoli, cauliflower, chicken

Live food and food other than flakes are highly desirable additions to your fish's diet, but remember to feed pellets or flakes as a staple. When you feed your fish table food, always serve it plain, not seasoned, salted or spiced.

likely carriers of disease. It is advised that you feed them to your fish only once or twice a month. While it is possible to culture tubifex at home, it isn't recommended, because it is very difficult and not worth the risk.

WHITEWORMS

These white or beige worms are also known as microworms. You can buy them from your dealer in serving-size amounts, or you can culture them at home. Starter kits can be obtained from pet dealers or ordered

by mail. It is best to feed these worms in small quantities to your fish because some aquarists believe that they can be fattening and constipating.

DAPHNIA

Daphnia are also referred to as water fleas. They constitute another excellent live food for your fish. *Daphnia* should only be fed every now and then to your fish because they can act as a laxative causing serious digestive problems. You can buy *Daphnia* from your local pet store or easily culture them at home.

DROSOPHILA

Drosophila are the larvae of the wingless fruit fly. Like the other live foods, you can sometimes buy them from the pet store or you can culture them at home.

BLOODWORMS

Also known as two-winged fly larvae, these are usually in good supply year-round and can be purchased at your pet store. They are very difficult to cultivate at home.

Of course, the live food category includes small fish as well as the animals listed above. Fish are used to feed large predatory fish that will

not be in the average community aquarium, and accordingly, the new aquarist need not be concerned with obtaining fish as fish food.

Frozen or Freeze-dried Foods

Frozen or freeze-dried foods offer the best of the live food without the risk of disease and without the hassle of preparing cultures. These include many of the live foods outlined above: brine shrimp, tubifex worms, *Daphnia* and bloodworms. In addition, mosquito larvae and krill are also available to the aquarist in this form. Frozen and freeze-dried foods are a great convenience to the hobbyist who wants to provide variety without having to purchase or culture live foods.

Table or Household Foods

Fresh, frozen or canned oysters, clams, mussels, crabmeat, lobster or bits of raw fish are fine, but do not offer canned tuna fish. Baked or boiled beans, steamed cauliflower or broccoli and boiled or baked potatoes are excellent additions to your herbivore's diet. Fresh spinach or

A carefully planned aquarium will house fish that feed and dwell at all levels of the tank.

lettuce is also good for your omnivorous and herbivorous fish. Carnivores will especially enjoy small bits of ground beef or cooked chicken.

These foods must be given in moderation. Remember, you are augmenting your fish's diet with these foods, not creating a staple. Household foods must be diced or shredded so that your fish can eat them. Don't offer your fish table scraps other than those listed above. Do not offer any bits of meat or vegetable that have been seasoned or spiced; table food needs to be plain and well-diced.

HOW TO FEED YOUR FISH

The biggest problems faced by the fish keeper are determining how much and how often to feed the fish. Some fish are gluttons, while others will stop eating when they are sated. In general, many experts believe that it is better to feed too little to your fish than to feed too much. Follow the guidelines listed below when feeding your fish, and you will develop a working sense of how much and how often to feed them.

1. Offer as much food as your fish will eat in five minutes. Flakes should sink no deeper than one-third the height of the tank; provide tablets or pellets for bottom-dwelling fish.

2. Feed your fish in very small portions over the five-minute period.

3. If you are home during the day, feed your fish over the course of the day in small portions. If you are not home, feed you fish twice a day at the same times every day—once in the morning, once at night.

4. Always feed your fish at the same spot in the tank.

5. Don't overfeed the fish, no matter how much you think they need more food. Overeating will stress your fish and cause detritus to accumulate in the tank, degrading water quality.

Watch all your fish during feeding, making sure that each gets its share of food. Remember that fish have different mouth shapes that allow them to feed at different levels in the tank. Some species will not go to the surface to eat and will wait

Oscars have a hefty appetite, so be sure not to overfeed them. (Red Tiger Oscars)

for food to disperse throughout the tank. Don't rely on surface feedings and the leftovers of others to feed bottom fish. Pellets that sink to the bottom should be provided for these fish. Remember, refusal to eat is one of the first signs of illness, so keep an eye out for fish that seem to have no interest in food.

Try not to feed your fish right after turning on the light; they won't be fully alert until about thirty minutes later. In addition, don't crumble the flake food. This will add fine particles to the water that are not ingested and that remain in the water degrading water quality. Your fish won't have any problems biting and grinding whole flake food.

If you are going to be away from your aquarium for a few days, the fish will be fine without food. For extended periods, make arrangements for someone to feed your fish or install an automatic food dispenser. If you choose the latter, be sure not to overload the dispenser, and set a long interval between feeding times so the fish will eat all that is offered.

CHAPTER SEVEN

To Good Health

Blue Gourami

Freshwater tropical fish are subject to all kinds of maladies. Pathogenic organisms including parasites, bacteria and viruses are present in all aquariums. Many are introduced with new fish and many are highly contagious. However, whether or not diseases actually break out depends on the resistance of your fish. Poor living conditions will weaken your fish, cause chronic stress and ultimately lower the fish's resistance. The importance of maintaining a healthy aquarium for your pets cannot be stressed too strongly. Even if you do everything in your power to maintain a disease-free aquarium, you still may find yourself confronting health conditions in your fish; even experts fall victim to these problems.

SIGNS OF ILLNESS

The first step in treating any kind of ailment in your aquarium is to recognize and identify the problem. You will be able to determine that a fish is not healthy by its appearance

*The close prox-
imity of fish in
an aquarium
necessitates the
use of a hospital
tank to stop the
spread of disease.
(Elongate Jewel
Cichlid)*

and its behavior. Because you have been spending time examining your fish while you feed them, you will be able to identify problems as soon as they manifest themselves. Telltale behavioral symptoms include: no desire to eat, hyperventilation of the gills, gasping for air near the surface, erratic swimming behavior, lack of movement, rubbing of body or fins, and twitching of fins.

External symptoms include a variety of physical abnormalities of the head, body, fins, gills, scales and anus. The symptoms of various diseases are outlined in the chart on pages 84–85.

THE HOSPITAL TANK

Many experts recommend that you set up a hospital tank to isolate individuals that are suffering from disease. This tank will reduce the likelihood of the disease spreading to others in the aquarium. It will provide refuge to an ailing fish that may be harassed by healthier fish. The hospital tank will make it easier to treat the fish without subjecting other fish to the treatment. And it will make it easier to observe and diagnose the ailing fish.

As your expertise in this hobby increases, and you start to accumulate more expensive fish, a hospital tank will be mandatory. It will also act as a quarantine tank, provided that it has not recently housed a diseased fish.

The hospital tank need not be large; a 10-gallon tank will do. It does need adequate filtration and aeration, but plants and gravel should be left out. Try to provide some kind of cover for the fish in the form of rocks or flower pots as a source of security.

TREATMENTS

It is very important that beginners use commercially available treatments instead of homemade remedies. Some experts recommend chemicals like malachite green or potassium permanganate. These chemicals must be handled in very exact dosages. If a fish is overdosed with one of them, it will kill the fish faster than the disease would have. Discuss all the possible remedies for a disease with your local pet dealer, and let that person advise you on the best commercial remedies that the store carries. If you are still not

satisfied, don't be afraid to call your veterinarian and ask a few questions. If your veterinarian does not treat fish, he or she can usually recommend somebody who does. Finally, when you apply the remedy, make sure that you follow the directions exactly.

The Old-fashioned Salt Bath

This is the most time-tested cure-all of the fish world. Sometimes called the progressive saltwater treatment, it is the most common use of the hospital tank. This very simple treatment has been known to cure a number of fish diseases including ich, fungus, velvet and tail rot. Many experts swear by it.

You simply add 1 teaspoon of table salt (not iodized) for each gallon of water to the hospital tank that houses your fish. Add the same amount of salt that night and twice the next day, again in the morning and at night. If you see no improvements by the third or fourth day, add 1 more teaspoon of salt each day. On the ninth and tenth days, make progressive water changes and check for results.

Emergency Cleaning

An emergency cleaning is the most severe treatment any tank can get. If any of the infestations in the chart at the end of this chapter strike more than three or four fish, you need to take drastic measures and perform an emergency cleaning. Place all the fish in the hospital tank and begin treatment. Then, turn your attention to the aquarium.

This very simply involves starting your aquarium from scratch. It must be thoroughly cleaned and totally restarted. Throw out filter media and save as little as possible. Empty out the contents of the tank. Wash the walls, the gravel and the filter with bleach. Of course, make sure that you rinse everything thoroughly. Do the same to the plastic plants. Throw out the rocks and buy new ones. If you have any live plants, dispose of them, too, and don't use them for any other purpose. Replace the filter media and airstones. Take the heater and wash it with bleach as well, making sure to rinse it thoroughly. In essence, you are starting over again because your tank was overrun by disease.

COMMON CONDITIONS

There are literally hundreds of possible maladies that can afflict fish. Some are specific to certain species and some can easily be transferred between species. Not all are common in the average home aquarium. The causes of common aquarium ailments may be bacteria, viruses, fungi or parasites. The following chart provides a general overview of those diseases you are most likely to encounter in your aquarium. If you observe your fish suffering from any of these symptoms, you should contact your veterinarian or pet dealer for assistance. The references in chapter 9 will also provide information on tropical fish diseases and their treatments.

DISEASE	SYMPTOMS
ANCHOR WORM	A white worm protrudes from a red agitated area on the fish's body. Infested fish rubs against anything it can, attempting to scratch off the parasite.
BODY SLIME FUNGUS	The protective skin mucus grows white and starts peeling off, as if the fish were shedding or molting. The fins are eventually covered as well.
CHINA DISEASE	Tail fins and other fins begin to fray, beginning at the base of the fin and working their way outward. Infected areas begin to blacken. Ventral region begins to turn black.
CONSTIPATION, INDIGESTION	Fish very inactive, usually rests on bottom of the tank. Abdominal swelling and bulging is likely to occur.
DROPSY (KIDNEY BLOAT)	The abdomen bloats noticeably, and the scales stick out like pinecones.
FIN OR TAIL ROT	Fins have missing parts, eventually become shredded. Rays become inflamed and entire fin may be eaten away.
FISH LICE	Round, disk-shaped, transparent crustaceans that clamp onto host and refuse to let go. Infected fish will rub against objects in the tank in an effort to remove the parasites.
FISH POX	Whitish or pinkish waxy film develops over fish's skin and fins.
FUNGUS	Fuzzy growth, different from velvet because it is more whitish in coloration.
FURUNCULOSIS	Raised bumps under the scales that eventually rupture and cause bleeding ulcers.

DISEASE	SYMPTOMS
GILL FLUKE	Gills swell pink and red; fish spends time at the surface gasping for air. Puslike fluid will be exuded from the gills.
HOLE-IN-THE-HEAD	The fish has white stringy feces and enlarged pus-filled sensory pores in the head. Also, erosion of the skin and muscles that eventually extends to the bones and skull.
ICH	Raised white spots about the size of a salt granule appear on the body and fins.
LEECHES	Long wormlike parasites attached at both ends to the fish that do not come off easily.
MOUTH FUNGUS	White cottony growth on mouth, sometimes spreading to the gills and other parts.
POP-EYE	Fish's eyes protrude from an inflamed eye socket.
SKIN FLUKE	Localized swelled areas, excessive mucus and ulcerations on skin. The fish is constantly trying to rid itself of these parasites by rubbing against aquarium objects.
SWIM BLADDER DISEASE	Fish swim on their sides, upside down, or somersault through the water. They can be found either on the top or the bottom of the tank.
TUMORS	Obvious bumps, lumps, protrusions that sometimes look like a large blister or wart.
ULCERS	Large red lesions, boils, dark reddening and bleeding.
VELVET	Fuzzy area grows with a yellow or golden color.

CHAPTER EIGHT

Resources

Home aquarists throughout the world number in the millions. As long as you have an aquarium, you will never be alone in this hobby. As you become more involved in aquarium keeping, you will be surprised at how many people share this avocation. You will find yourself going to your local pet dealer just to see new fish arrivals, to talk about aquarium problems and to exchange ideas with fellow aquarists. You will be sure to pick up some of the most valuable information on fish keeping from amateurs who enjoy the thrills of this hobby.

CLUBS

In many areas, aquarium enthusiasts have formed clubs and associations where ideas and techniques are endlessly bantered about. Find these organizations by asking your local pet dealer if one exists in your area. Not only are these organizations great for gathering information, but they may also help you find and buy used equipment as well as healthy homebred fish.

BOOKS

Literally thousands of books have been published on every facet of aquarium keeping. The recommended reading in this book (chapter 9) is a mere smattering of what is available for the new and experienced aquarist. Each one of the books listed has its own bibliography, which will help you to delve further into the field. Books have been written to address virtually every aspect of the hobby. They cover broad topics, like basic aquarium setup, to very specialized topics, like the proper husbandry of a certain species. If you have any questions about aquarium keeping, they are covered in a book.

MAGAZINES

Monthly aquarium magazines provide you with some of the most up-to-date information on aquarium keeping. Timely articles on breeding, feeding, disease and species specific husbandry will both entertain and inform the new aquarist. Product information and classified advertising are excellent features of the aquarium magazine. Two such magazines that have proven to be very good conduits of information are *Aquarium Fish Magazine* (P.O. Box 53351, Boulder, CO 80322; 303-666-8504) and *Tropical Fish Hobbyist* (One TFH Plaza, Neptune City, NJ 07753; 732-988-8400).

FISH ON THE INTERNET

Yes, even fish keeping has entered the computer age. Going online is probably the fastest way to obtain and exchange information on aquarium keeping. If you have access to the Internet, then you have unlimited access to a vast amount of information on this hobby. Some Internet access companies have even established networks for fish enthusiasts. One such network is Fishnet by CompuServe (800-524-3388). Membership in this network gives you access to hobbyists, professional aquarists, researchers, breeders and vendors of aquarium products. You can even get immediate advice from the staff about sick fish.

This is just one example of what is available to the aquarist on the Internet. There are also bulletin board systems and mailing lists for aquarists, and some experts and vendors have home pages on the Internet. Any good search machine will help you access these resources.

CHAPTER NINE

Recommended Reading

Alderton, David. *The International Encyclopedia of Tropical Freshwater Fish.* New York: Howell Book House, 1997.

Axelrod, H. R. *Tropical Fish as a New Pet.* Neptune City, N.J.: TFH Publications, Inc., 1991.

————. *Encyclopedia of Tropical Fishes: With Special Emphasis on Techniques of Breeding.* Neptune City, N.J.: TFH Publications, Inc., 1986.

Axelrod, H. R. and L. P. Schultz. *Handbook of Tropical Aquarium Fishes.* Neptune City, N.J.: TFH Publications, Inc., 1990.

Bailey, M. and G. Sandford. *The Ultimate Aquarium.* New York: Smithmark Publishers, 1995.

DeVito, C. and G. Skomal. *The Goldfish: An Owner's Guide to a Happy Healthy Pet.* New York: Howell Book House, 1996.

Emmens, C. W. *Tropical Fish: A Complete Introduction.* Neptune City, N.J.: TFH Publications, Inc., 1987.

Eschmeyer, W. M. *Catalogue of the Genera of Recent Fishes.* San Francisco: California Academy of Sciences, 1990.

Freise, U. E. *Aquarium Fish.* Neptune City, N.J.: TFH Publications Inc., 1989.

Halstead, B. W. and B. L. Landa. *Tropical Fish.* New York: Golden Press, 1985.

James, B. *A Fishkeeper's Guide to Aquarium Plants.* London: Salamander Books, 1986.

Mills, D. *Aquarium Fish.* New York: Dorling Kindersley Publishing, 1993.

Moyle, P. B. and J. J. Cech, Jr. *Fishes: An Introduction to Ichthyology.* Englewood Cliffs, N.J.: Prentice-Hall Inc., 1982.

Sandford, G. *An Illustrated Encyclopedia of Aquarium Fish.* New York: Howell Book House, 1995.

Scheurmann, I. *The New Aquarium Handbook.* Hauppauge, N.Y.: Barron's Educational Series, Inc., 1986.

———. *Water Plants in the Aquarium.* Hauppauge, N.Y.: Barron's Educational Series, Inc., 1987.

Scott, P. W. *The Complete Aquarium.* New York: Dorling Kindersley Publishing, 1995.

Stadelmann, P. *Tropical Fish: A Complete Pet Owner's Manual.* Hauppauge, N.Y.: Barron's Educational Series, Inc., 1991.

Stoskopf, M. K. *Fish Medicine.* Philadelphia: W.B. Saunders Co., 1993.

Acidity level (pH), 15, 35
Aeration, 13, 15, 16, 20–21
Air hoses, 21
Air pumps, 20–21
Airstones, 20, 21
Algae, 40–42
Algal sponges, 31
American knifefish, 52
Anatomy of fish, 6
Anchor worms, 84
Angelfish, 4, 5, 49, 61–62, 73
Aquariums, 11–37. *See also*
   Tanks; *specific topics*
   adding fish to, 36–37, 55
   maintenance, 39–46
   maturation, 34–36, 42
   setting up, 32–34
Arched Corydoras, 63
Armored catfish, 48–49
Arowana, 70–71
Artificial plants, 26
Attributes of fish, 2–5
Axelrod's Corydoras, 63–64

Banded knifefish, 52
Barbs, 48, 59–60, 68–69
Beginners, fish for, 53–65
   fish to avoid, 65–71
Belontiidae, 50–51, 59, 62
Bettas, 51, 59
Biological filtration, 16, 19–20
Biology of fish, 2–5, 48
Black Mollies, 56–57, 62
Black Neon Tetras, 61
Bloodworms, 76
Blue Gouramis, 62
Body slime fungus, 84
Bottom fish, 5, 8, 25, 40, 63–65
Breeding, 9, 48
Brine shrimp, 75

Bronze Corydoras, 63
Bunch plants, 27

Captivity, fish in, 8–9
Carbon dioxide, 6, 15, 16, 21, 26, 27
Cardinal Tetras, 47–48, 61
Carnivores, 72–74, 78
Catfish, 8, 41, 48–49, 63, 65
Characins, 49, 59, 61, 68
Chemical filtration, 16–19
China disease, 84
Choosing fish, 53–71
Cichlids, 49–50, 61–62, 66–68
Cleaning, 39–46
   emergency, 83
   supplies, 31–32
Clown Knifefish, 70
Clown Loaches, 48, 64
Clown Plecostomus, 65
Cobitidae, 48, 64
Commercial foods, 74–75
Community tanks, 10, 25, 53–55
   right fish for, 53–65
Constipation, 84
Coral sand, 25
Corydoras catfish, 49, 63–64
Cyprinids, 48, 57–61, 64, 65, 68–69

Daily maintenance, 45
Danios, 57–58
Daphnia, 76
Day's Spinetail Gouramis, 53
Dealers, 10
   bringing fish home from, 35, 36
   selection of fish at, 54–55

Decorations, tank, 29–30
Discus, 49
Diseases. *See* Illnesses
Dried foods, 74–75
Dropsy, 84
Drosophila, 76
Dusky Corydoras, 64
Dwarf Gouramis, 62

Ears, 7
Earthworms, 75
Egglayers, 48
Elephantnose, 52
Emergency cleaning, 83
Evolution of fish, 1–2
External power filters, 18–19, 40
Eyes, 7

Families of fish, 47–71
Feeding, 5, 78–79. *See also* Food
   amount and frequency of, 78–79
   strategies, 72–74
Fertilization, of live plants, 28
Filter systems, 16–21, 40
Fins, 2–3, 6
Fin rot, 84
Fish keeper, responsibilities of, 9–10
Fish lice, 84
Fishnets, 31
Fish pox, 84
Flake foods, 74–75
Floating plants, 27
Flying Fox, 64
Food, 74–78
Frozen foods, 76, 77
Fungus, 84, 85
Furunculosis, 84

Gill fluke, 85
Gills, 6
Glass Catfish, 63
Glowlight Tetra, 61
Goldfish, 8, 12, 22, 73
Gouramis, 51, 53, 62
Gravel, 25–26
Green Discus, 66–67
Green Swordtail, 56
Guppies, 55, 56, 73

Hardness, water, 15, 16, 25, 35
Hatchetfish, 58
Health concerns. *See* Illnesses
Heaters, 21–23
Herbivores, 73, 74, 78
Hole-in-the-head disease, 85
Hood of aquarium, 14
Hospital tanks, 81–83
Household foods, 76, 77–78

Ich, 85
Illnesses, 80–85
    common conditions, 83
    symptoms, 80–81, 84–85
    treatments, 82–83
Incompatibility of fish, 54
Indigestion, 84
Insectivores, 73
Internal box filter, 18
Internet sources, 87

Jack Dempsey, 49, 68
Jewel Cichlid, 67–68

Kidney bloat, 84
Killifish, 50
Kissing Fish, 51
Knifefish, 52, 70
Krill, 77

Labyrinth fish, 50–51
Lateral line, 6, 8

Leeches, 85
Leopard Corydoras, 64
Lighting, aquarium, 23–24
Livebearers, 48
Live foods, 75–77
Live plants, 26–29, 73
Loaches, 48, 69

Magazines, 87
Maintenance, 39–46
Malachite green, 82
Marbled Hatchetfish, 58
Maturation, 34–36, 42
Mechanical filtration, 16–17,
    19
Mexican Molly, 56
Microworms, 76
Midwater fish, 59–63
Mollies, 56–57, 62
Monthly maintenance, 45
Mormyrids, 52
Mosquito larvae, 77
Mouth, 5, 78
Mouth fungus, 85
Mudskippers, 70
Mulm, 39

Nares, 7
Neon Tetras, 5, 12, 47–49,
    61–62
"New tank syndrome," 35–36
Nitrogen cycle, 16, 17, 35, 39
Nutrition, 72–79

Omnivores, 73–74, 78
Oscars, 5, 49, 67, 79
Oxygen, 6, 12
    aeration and, 20–21

Paradise Fish, 51, 62
Pearl Danios, 58
Pearl Gouramis, 62
Pet stores. *See* Dealers

pH (acidity level), 15, 35
Piranhas, 49, 73
Piston air pumps, 21
Plants, 26–29
Platy, 57
Pop-eye, 85
Pumps, 20–21

Quarantine tanks, 37

Rainbowfish, 51
Rasboras, 48, 60–61
Red-bellied Piranhas, 49
Red Devils, 67
Red Rasboras, 60–61
Red Snakeheads, 69
Red-tailed Sharks, 48, 65
Resources, 86–87
Responsibilities of fish keeper,
    9–10
Rosy Barbs, 59–60
Ruby Barbs, 60
Runny-nose Tetras, 68

Sailfin Plecos, 40
Salt baths, 82
Scales, 4, 6
Screens, aquarium, 32
Senses, 6–8
Setting up aquarium, 32–34
Siamese Fighting Fish, 51, 59
Sight, 7
Silver Hatchetfish, 58
Siphons, 43–45
Skin fluke, 85
Sludgeworms, 75–76
Smell, 7–8
Snakeskin Gouramis, 62
Sound, 7
Species of fish, 47–71
Species tanks, 53, 71
Specimen plants, 27
Speckled knifefish, 52

Splendid Rainbows, 51
Spotted Puffers, 72
Stands, aquarium, 13–14
Stress, fish, 35, 38–39
Sucking Loaches, 69
Surface area of tank, 12, 13
Surface feedings, 79
Swim bladder, 4–6
Swim bladder disease, 85
Symptoms of diseases, 80–81, 84–85

Table foods, 76, 77–78
Tail rot, 84
Tanks, 11. *See also* Water
    adding fish to, 36–37, 55
    aeration, 13, 15, 16, 20–21
    avoid direct sunlight, 11
    cleaning supplies, 31
    community, 10, 25, 53–55
    decorations for, 29–30
    emergency cleaning, 83
    filter systems, 16–21
    gravel, 25–26
    heaters, 21–23
    hospital, 81–83
    lighting of, 23–24
    maturation of, 34–36, 42
    monitoring fish in, 38–39

"new tank syndrome," 35–36
    number of fish for, 12
    plants for, 26–29
    quarantine, 37
    selection of, 12–13, 33
    setting up, 32–34
    size of, 12–13, 33
    species, 53, 71
    surface area of, 12, 13
    test kits, 15, 30–31
    weight of full, 11
Taste, 8
Temperature of water, 12, 15, 21–23
Test kits, water, 15, 30–31
Tetras, 47–48, 61, 68. *See also* Neon Tetras
Thermometers, 23
Tiger Barbs, 48, 60
Tinfoil Barbs, 68–69
Topwater fish, 54, 55–59
Touch, 8
Treatments, 82–83
Tubifex, 75–76
Tumors, 85

Ulcers, 85
Undergravel filters, 19–20, 25

Vacuuming, 39–40
Vacuums, 31, 39
Variable Platy, 57
Velvet, 85

Water, 14–23
    aeration, 13, 15, 16, 20–21
    changing, 43–45
    conditioning of, 34–36
    hardness, 15, 16, 25, 35
    heaters, 21–23
    maturation, 34–36, 42
    nitrogen cycle and, 16, 17
    oxygen content, 15
    pH of, 15, 35
    temperature of, 12, 15, 21–22
    testing, 42–43
    test kits, 15, 30–31
Water fleas, 76
Weekly maintenance, 45
White Cloud Mountain Minnows, 58
Whiteworms, 76
"Window cleaning" fish, 65

Zebra Danio, 48, 57–58